A Guide to Software Quality Engineering

In today's fast-paced digital world, delivering high-quality software is not just a goal; it's an absolute necessity. *A Guide to Software Quality Engineering* is a companion book for anyone involved in software development, testing, or quality assurance.

This comprehensive book takes you on a transformative journey through the world of software quality engineering, providing invaluable insights, practical methodologies, and expert advice that will elevate your projects to new levels of excellence.

The book features the following points:

- Performance Testing Security Testing
- Usability Testing
- Continuous Integration and Continuous Testing
- Requirements Engineering and Quality
- Code Quality and Static Analysis
- Defect Management and Root Cause Analysis
- Release and Deployment Management

Dive into the fundamental principles of software quality engineering, understanding the critical role it plays in ensuring customer satisfaction, user experience, and the overall success of your software products. Whether you're a seasoned professional or a budding enthusiast, this book caters to all levels of expertise.

Shravan Pargaonkar is a seasoned expert in the field of software quality engineering, with over 7 years of hands-on experience in developing, testing, and ensuring the highest standards of software excellence. As a passionate advocate for quality-driven development, Shravan has been at the forefront of innovative practices, guiding numerous organizations toward successful software projects and delighted customers. With a strong background in and a natural flair for problem-solving, Shravan's journey in software quality engineering began early in his career. His diverse professional experiences, ranging from startups to multinational corporations, have provided him with unique insights into the challenges faced by software development teams across different industries.

A Guide to Software Quality Engineering

Shravan Pargaonkar

CRC Press
Taylor & Francis Group
Boca Raton London New York

CRC Press is an imprint of the
Taylor & Francis Group, an **informa** business

AN AUERBACH BOOK

First edition published 2024
by CRC Press
2385 NW Executive Center Drive, Suite 320, Boca Raton FL 33431

and by CRC Press
4 Park Square, Milton Park, Abingdon, Oxon, OX14 4RN

CRC Press is an imprint of Taylor & Francis Group, LLC

ISBN: 978-1-032-69441-2 (hbk)
ISBN: 978-1-032-69301-9 (pbk)
ISBN: 978-1-032-70204-9 (ebk)

DOI: 10.1201/9781032702049

Typeset in Caslon
by MPS Limited, Dehradun

This book is dedicated to each and every one of you, who contributes to the advancement of software quality engineering, making a positive impact on the world of software development.

To our friends, families, and other loved ones who support us in our pursuit of excellence, understanding the dedication and long hours that go into ensuring software quality.

This book is dedicated to all the passionate software quality engineers, testers, and professionals who strive for excellence in their work.

To the individuals who continuously push the boundaries of software quality engineering, embracing new methodologies, tools, and practices to deliver high-quality software.

To the teams that collaborate and support each other, valuing open communication, knowledge sharing, and a shared commitment to delivering software that meets and exceeds customer expectations.

To the leaders who champion a culture of quality, recognizing the critical role that software quality engineering plays in achieving organizational success.

To the educators and mentors who inspire and guide the next generation of quality engineers, imparting knowledge, and experience, and instilling a passion for continuous improvement.

To the customers and end-users who provide valuable feedback and inspire us to continually enhance the quality of our software products.

Thank you all for your unwavering commitment to quality and for inspiring us to continually strive for excellence.

Contents

1

INTRODUCTION TO SOFTWARE QUALITY ENGINEERING

Software quality engineering is the art of creating software systems that not only meet specified requirements but also surpass user expectations. Achieving exceptional software quality requires a delicate balance of various crucial aspects, including functionality, reliability, usability, performance, security, and maintainability. By prioritizing software quality, we guarantee customer satisfaction, mitigate potential risks, and optimize the overall value of our software products.

Now, let's delve into the pivotal dimensions that constitute software quality.

1.1 Understanding Software Quality

1.1.1 Functionality

This dimension centers around ensuring that the software fulfills its intended purpose and performs its designated functions effectively and accurately.

1.1.2 Reliability

Reliability pertains to the software's ability to operate consistently and predictably under specific conditions without encountering failures or errors.

1.1.3 Usability

Usability refers to how seamlessly and efficiently users can interact with the software, encompassing aspects like user interface design, accessibility, and the overall user experience.

DOI: 10.1201/9781032702049-1

1.1.4 Performance

Performance deals with the software's speed, responsiveness, scalability, and resource utilization in meeting specified performance requirements.

1.1.5 Security

Security involves safeguarding the software and its data from unauthorized access, vulnerabilities, and potential threats.

1.1.6 Maintainability

Maintainability focuses on how easily the software can be modified, enhanced, or repaired to address defects, incorporate new features, or adapt to changing requirements.

1.1.7 Testability

Testability assesses how well the software can be tested and the extent to which defects can be identified and isolated efficiently.

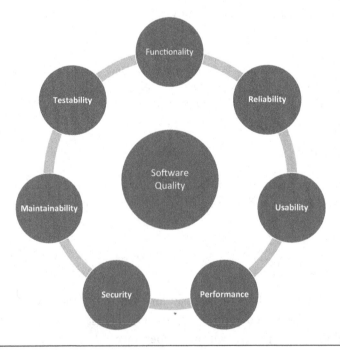

Dimensions of software quality.

1.2 Importance of Software Quality Engineering

Software quality engineering plays a pivotal role in ensuring that software products meet the desired levels of excellence. It involves a systematic and disciplined approach to evaluating, enhancing, and maintaining software quality throughout the entire software development life cycle (SDLC).

1.2.1 Customer Satisfaction

High-quality software not only meets customer expectations but also results in increased satisfaction and loyalty. Quality engineering practices, such as rigorous testing and continuous improvement, help deliver software that not only meets but often surpasses customer needs.

1.2.2 Risk Mitigation

Software defects and failures can lead to financial losses, reputational damage, and even safety hazards. Quality engineering helps mitigate these risks by identifying and addressing issues early in the development process, reducing the likelihood of costly errors in the final product.

1.2.3 Cost Optimization

Fixing defects in later stages of the SDLC can be time-consuming and expensive. By focusing on quality from the outset, organizations can reduce rework, improve efficiency, and minimize costs associated with software defects, ultimately leading to better resource allocation.

1.2.4 Competitive Advantage

In today's competitive landscape, high-quality software can differentiate an organization from its rivals. By consistently delivering reliable, user-friendly, and secure software, companies can gain a competitive edge and stand out in the market.

1.3 Evolution of Software Quality Engineering

Software quality engineering has undergone significant evolution in response to changing industry practices and technological advancements. Understanding this evolution provides valuable insights into the current state and future directions of quality engineering.

1.3.1 Waterfall Model

In the early days, quality assurance primarily focused on end-of-life testing, with the waterfall model dominating as the primary SDLC approach. Quality activities were mostly conducted in the testing phase, often resulting in late defect detection and limited opportunities for feedback and improvement.

1.3.2 Shift to Quality Assurance

Recognizing the importance of quality, the role of quality assurance expanded beyond testing. Quality engineers started engaging in earlier stages of the SDLC, including requirements engineering, design reviews, and process improvement, promoting a proactive approach to quality.

1.3.3 Agile and Iterative Approaches

The advent of agile methodologies brought about a significant shift in quality engineering practices. Iterative development, continuous integration, and test-driven development gained popularity, enabling faster feedback cycles and greater collaboration between development and testing teams.

1.3.4 DevOps and Continuous Testing

The integration of development and operations gave rise to DevOps practices, where continuous testing became integral. Emphasizing automated testing, infrastructure as code, and monitoring in production environments, this shift further enhanced the software quality engineering process.

1.4 Software Engineering Fundamentals

Software Engineering is a systematic and disciplined approach to designing, developing, testing, deploying, and maintaining software systems. It involves the application of engineering principles, methods, and techniques to create high-quality software products that meet user needs, adhere to specifications, and are completed within defined time and budget constraints. Let's explore the key aspects of software engineering in detail.

1.4.1 Systematic Approach

Software engineering emphasizes the need for a structured and organized approach to software development. It involves breaking down the entire process into manageable phases and tasks, ensuring that each step is well-defined, documented, and followed consistently.

1.4.2 Requirements Engineering

One of the initial steps in software engineering is gathering and analyzing user requirements. This involves understanding what the software should do, its functionalities, user expectations, and any constraints. Clear and accurate requirements serve as the foundation for the entire development process.

1.4.3 Design

Once the requirements are established, the design phase focuses on creating a blueprint for the software. This includes architectural design, which outlines the overall structure of the system, and detailed design, which defines how individual components and modules will work together.

1.4.4 Implementation and Coding

In this phase, developers write the actual code based on the design specifications. Coding follows coding standards and best practices and often involves using programming languages, libraries, and frameworks.

1.4.5 Testing

Testing is a critical aspect of software engineering. It involves systematically evaluating the software to identify defects, inconsistencies, and performance issues. Effective testing, ranging from unit testing to user acceptance testing, is essential for validating software quality.

1.4.6 Deployment and Maintenance

After successful testing, the software is deployed to the production environment. However, software engineering doesn't stop here. Maintenance involves continuous monitoring, bug fixing, updates, and enhancements to ensure that the software remains reliable, secure, and aligned with evolving user needs.

1.4.7 Project Management

Software engineering projects require effective project management to ensure that they are completed within budget and on schedule. This includes task scheduling, resource allocation, risk management, and communication among team members and stakeholders.

1.4.8 Quality Assurance

Quality is a cornerstone of software engineering. QA practices involve implementing processes and measures to ensure that the software meets the highest standards. This includes adherence to coding standards, best practices, and comprehensive testing.

1.4.9 Documentation

Documentation is essential to ensure that the software can be understood, maintained, and improved over time. Software engineering involves creating various documentation types, such as requirement documents, design documents, user manuals, and technical documentation.

1.4.10 Collaboration and Communication

Software engineering projects often involve collaboration among multidisciplinary teams, including developers, designers, testers, and domain experts. Effective communication among team members and stakeholders is crucial to ensure a shared understanding of project goals and requirements.

1.4.11 Ethical and Professional Considerations

Software engineers are responsible for creating products that impact users' lives and society as a whole. Ethical considerations, such as data privacy, security, and accessibility, play a significant role in software engineering practices.

1.5 The Linkage between Software Quality and Software Engineering

Software quality and software engineering are interconnected disciplines that work together to create dependable, efficient, and user-centric software systems. Software engineering provides the framework and methodologies for developing software, while software quality ensures that the end product meets the highest standards of excellence. Let us explore the crucial link between software quality and software engineering.

1.5.1 Foundation of Quality in Software Engineering

Software engineering lays the foundation for achieving software quality. The systematic and structured approach of software engineering methodologies ensures that software is developed using well-defined processes, best practices, and industry standards. These methodologies, such as the Waterfall model, Agile, or DevOps, provide the structure for managing the development lifecycle, from requirements gathering to deployment and maintenance.

1.5.2 Quality Assurance through Software Engineering

Software engineering practices inherently include elements of quality assurance. By implementing coding standards, conducting thorough testing, and adhering to design principles, software engineering ensures that defects are identified and addressed early in the development process. This prevents defects from propagating through later stages, reducing the cost and effort required for corrections.

1.5.3 Incorporation of Quality Attributes

Software engineering methodologies consider various quality attributes that define software quality, such as functionality, reliability, usability, and performance. Design decisions made during the software engineering process directly influence these attributes. For instance, the architectural choices made during the design phase can impact the system's reliability and scalability.

1.5.4 Testing and Validation

Software engineering methodologies incorporate testing practices as a critical component of the development process. Rigorous testing, which is an integral part of software engineering, ensures that the software functions as intended and meets user requirements. Effective testing, ranging from unit testing to user acceptance testing, is essential for validating software quality.

1.5.5 Iterative Improvement

Both software quality and software engineering advocate for a culture of continuous improvement. Software engineering methodologies, like Agile, promote iterative development cycles, allowing for regular feedback and adjustments. This iterative approach aligns well with the concept of enhancing software quality over time by addressing issues, incorporating user feedback, and making improvements incrementally.

1.5.6 Process Efficiency and Quality

Software engineering methodologies emphasize process efficiency and optimization. By following well-defined processes, automating repetitive tasks, and implementing continuous integration and deployment practices, software engineering enhances both development speed and software quality. Automated testing, for example, is a software engineering practice that directly contributes to ensuring software quality by identifying defects quickly and consistently.

1.5.7 User-Centric Approach

Both software quality and software engineering prioritize user needs. Software engineering methodologies encourage close collaboration with stakeholders, ensuring that user requirements are accurately captured. By designing software with the end user in mind, software engineering contributes to achieving high user satisfaction and overall software quality.

1.5.8 Conclusion

The relationship between software quality and software engineering is symbiotic. Software engineering provides the framework and practices for creating software systems, while software quality ensures that those systems meet user expectations and adhere to quality attributes. The migration of software quality principles within the software engineering process leads to the development of dependable, efficient, and user-friendly software products that deliver value to users and stakeholders. Software engineering provides the structure, tools, and methodologies, while software quality ensures that the end result meets the highest standards of excellence.

1.6 Software Engineering Culture and Ethics

Software Engineering Culture: Software engineering culture encompasses the shared values, beliefs, practices, and behaviors that define how a software development team operates and produces high-quality software. It shapes the team's approach to collaboration, problem-solving, innovation, and communication. A strong software engineering culture contributes to efficient development processes, improved software quality, and a positive work environment. Let's explore key aspects of software engineering culture.

1.6.1 Collaboration

A culture of collaboration encourages team members to work together, share knowledge, and contribute their expertise. Cross-functional teams with diverse skills foster creativity and faster problem-solving.

1.6.2 Continuous Learning

Embracing a culture of continuous learning promotes staying updated with new technologies, best practices, and industry trends. Encouraging skill development enhances the team's capabilities and the quality of their work.

1.6.3 Agility

An agile culture values adaptability, quick iterations, and responsiveness to changing requirements. Agile methodologies like Scrum and Kanban promote flexibility and customer collaboration throughout the development lifecycle.

1.6.4 Innovation

A culture that encourages innovation fosters creativity and new ideas. Creating an environment where team members are comfortable experimenting and proposing novel solutions can lead to breakthrough innovations.

1.6.5 Quality Focus

Prioritizing software quality in the culture results in consistent testing, code reviews, and adherence to coding standards. Quality becomes a collective responsibility rather than an afterthought.

1.6.6 Communication

Open and transparent communication is essential for effective collaboration. Regular meetings, stand-ups, and clear documentation ensure that everyone is aligned and informed.

Software Engineering Ethics: Ethics in software engineering involves considering the moral implications of technology decisions and actions.

1.6.7 Privacy

Software engineers must respect users' privacy by designing systems that handle sensitive data securely and obtain user consent for data collection and usage.

1.6.8 Accessibility

Developing software that is accessible to all, including people with disabilities, ensures inclusivity and equal access to technology.

1.6.9 Security

Ethical software engineering involves implementing robust security measures to protect user data from breaches and cyber threats.

1.6.10 Transparency

Being transparent about data usage, algorithms, and potential biases in software applications fosters trust and accountability.

1.6.11 Intellectual Property

Respecting intellectual property rights and licenses when using third-party libraries, frameworks, and open-source software is crucial.

1.6.12 Social Impact

Consider the potential social, economic, and environmental impacts of software products. Avoid creating technologies that could harm society or exploit vulnerable populations.

1.6.13 Honesty

Ethical software engineers are honest about the limitations and risks of their software, even if it means admitting flaws or limitations.

1.6.14 Ethics in software quality engineering

Software engineers have a responsibility to ensure that their work upholds ethical standards, respects users' rights, and contributes positively to society. This chapter contains some key ethical considerations.

1.6.15 Conclusion

A strong software engineering culture is rooted in collaboration, learning, innovation, and a focus on quality. Ethical considerations are an integral part of this culture, guiding decisions that impact users, society, and the environment. By fostering a positive software engineering culture and adhering to ethical principles, software engineers can create products that not only meet technical standards but also contribute positively to the world around them.

1.7 Value of Quality

The value of quality in software engineering extends beyond the immediate development process. It encompasses the benefits that high-quality software brings to users, stakeholders, and the organization as a whole. Quality software delivers both short-term advantages and long-term value.

1.7.1 Customer Satisfaction

High-quality software meets user expectations, resulting in improved customer satisfaction and loyalty. Satisfied users are more likely to recommend the software to others.

1.7.2 Reduced Defects

Quality software has fewer defects and requires fewer post-release fixes. This reduces maintenance costs and avoids disruptions for users.

1.7.3 Enhanced Reputation

Consistently delivering quality software builds a positive reputation for the organization, enhancing its credibility and market presence.

1.7.4 Efficient Operations

Quality software improves operational efficiency by minimizing downtime due to defects and reducing the need for manual interventions.

1.7.5 Lower Costs

While quality requires an investment upfront, it leads to lower overall costs in the long run due to reduced rework, support efforts, and customer complaints.

1.7.6 Competitive Advantage

High-quality software differentiates the organization from competitors, attracting more users and stakeholders.

1.7.7 Cost of Quality

The cost of quality encompasses both the visible and hidden expenses associated with ensuring software quality throughout its lifecycle. These costs can be categorizedinto four main types.

1.7.7.1 Prevention Costs Prevention costs are expenses incurred to prevent defects from occurring in the first place. They include the following:

- Training: Investing in training for developers and testers to improve skills and knowledge.
- Process Improvement: Initiatives to enhance development processes, reduce defects, and streamline workflows.
- Quality Planning: Activities to define quality standards, requirements, and processes.

1.7.7.2 Appraisal Costs   Appraisal costs are related to evaluating and verifying the software's quality. They include the following:

- Testing: Conducting various testing activities, such as unit testing, integration testing, and system testing.
- Inspections: Reviewing code, design, and documentation to identify defects and ensure adherence to standards.
- Quality Audits: Performing audits to assess compliance with quality processes and standards.

1.7.7.3 Internal Failure Costs   Internal failure costs arise when defects are identified and corrected before the software is released to customers. They include Bug Fixes: Correcting defects and issues found during testing and development. Rework: Revising code, design, or documentation to rectify errors.

1.7.7.4 External Failure Costs   External failure costs occur when defects are identified after the software is released and used by customers. They include the following:

- Customer Support: Addressing customer complaints, inquiries, and issues related to software defects.
- Reputation Damage: Costs associated with damage to the organization's reputation due to poor software quality.

1.7.8 Conclusion

Understanding the value and cost of quality in software engineering is crucial for making informed decisions. While investing in quality incurs certain costs upfront, the long-term benefits in terms of customer satisfaction, operational efficiency, and market competitiveness far outweigh these expenses. By prioritizing quality throughout the software development lifecycle, organizations can achieve sustainable growth, enhance their reputation, and deliver software that meets or exceeds user expectations.

1.8 Software Quality Models and Characteristics

Software quality models provide frameworks for evaluating and measuring the attributes that define high-quality software. These models offer guidelines and standards that help software developers and testers assess the various aspects of software quality. Let's explore some well-known software quality models and the characteristics they focus on.

1.8.1 ISO 25010

ISO 25010 is a comprehensive software quality model that covers a wide range of characteristics and sub-characteristics. It provides a structured framework for evaluating software quality. The model is divided into two main categories.

1.8.2 Functional Suitability

- Accuracy: The software's ability to provide accurate and correct results.
- Interoperability: How well the software interacts with other systems and components.
- Compliance: Adherence to specified standards, regulations, and requirements.

1.8.3 Performance Efficiency

- Time Behavior: The software's response time and processing speed.
- Resource Utilization: Efficient use of system resources like memory and CPU.
- Capacity: The software's ability to handle varying workloads and volumes.

1.8.4 Compatibility

- Coexistence: How well the software can work in conjunction with other software.
- Interoperability: Similar to the characteristic of functional suitability, focusing on compatibility with other systems.

1.8.5 Usability

- Understandability: The ease with which users can understand the software's functionalities.

- Operability: How user-friendly the software is, enabling users to perform tasks effectively.
- User Interface Aesthetics: The visual appeal and layout of the user interface.

1.8.6 Reliability

- Maturity: The software's stability and consistency over time.
- Fault Tolerance: The software's ability to continue functioning despite minor failures.
- Recoverability: The software's ability to recover from failures and restore normal operation.

1.8.7 Security

- Confidentiality: Protecting sensitive data from unauthorized access.
- Integrity: Ensuring the accuracy and consistency of data and information.
- Non-Repudiation: Preventing users from denying actions they've taken.

1.8.8 Maintainability

- Modularity: The software's ability to be divided into distinct modules for easier management.
- Reusability: The extent to which components can be reused in different contexts.
- Analyzability: The ease with which developers can analyze and identify issues in the code.

1.8.9 Portability

- Adaptability: The software's ability to be adapted to different environments and platforms.
- Install ability: The ease with which the software can be installed on various systems.
- Replaceability: The software's ability to be replaced by another similar software.

1.8.10 Capability Maturity Model Integration (CMMI)

CMMI is a process improvement model that focuses on the maturity and capability of an organization's processes rather than specific software characteristics. It has five levels of maturity, from Initial (Level 1) to Optimizing (Level 5). Higher maturity levels indicate better process capability, leading to improved software quality.

1.9 Conclusion

Software quality models provide structured frameworks for evaluating and improving software quality. ISO 25010 focuses on a wide range of characteristics, from functionality and performance to security and portability. CMMI emphasizes process maturity to enhance overall software quality. By utilizing these models, software development teams can systematically assess and address various dimensions of software quality, resulting in reliable, efficient, and user-centric software products.

1.8 CASE STUDY: ELTHE EVOLUTION OF SOFTWARE QUALITY AT TECH SOLUTIONS INC. CORPORATION

In this case study, we explore how Tech Solutions Inc. Corporation transformed its software quality engineering practices over time.

Example: Tech Solutions Inc. Corporation initially followed a waterfall approach, where quality assurance activities were confined to the testing phase. This resulted in late defect detection and costly rework. However, recognizing the need for improved quality, the organization adopted agile methodologies. Through iterative development and continuous collaboration between the development and testing teams, Tech Solutions Inc. Corporation achieved early defect detection and faster feedback cycles. Quality engineers actively participated in requirements refinement, design reviews, and regular testing, leading to improved software quality. With the adoption of DevOps practices, Tech Solutions Inc. Corporation further enhanced its quality engineering approach. Continuous testing was integrated into the deployment pipeline, enabling automated testing, instant feedback on code changes, and real-time monitoring of production systems. This shift resulted in higher customer satisfaction, reduced defect rates, and an accelerated time-to-market.

Practical Exercise:

- Reflect on your organization's software quality practices and identify areas for improvement. Consider the following questions.
- How involved are quality engineers in various stages of your organization's SDLC?
- Is there a strong focus on early defect detection and prevention?
- Are there any opportunities to introduce more automation and continuous testing practices?
- How effectively is customer satisfaction measured and incorporated into quality engineering processes?
- What steps can be taken to enhance collaboration between development, testing, and operations teams?
- By analyzing and addressing these aspects, you can formulate a roadmap for enhancing software quality engineering practices in your organization.
- In the next chapter, we will explore the key processes and activities involved in software quality engineering and how they can be applied to deliver high-quality software.

Note. This chapter introduces software quality engineering, highlighting its importance and evolution. Case studies and practical exercises are included to reinforce the concepts and encourage reflection. Subsequent chapters will dive deeper into specific aspects of quality engineering to provide a comprehensive understanding of the subject matter.

2

SOFTWARE DEVELOPMENT LIFE CYCLE AND QUALITY ENGINEERING

2.1 Overview of Software Development Life Cycle (SDLC) Models

The SDLC comprises the processes and activities involved in developing software systems. Various SDLC models exist, each offering its own approach and sequence of phases. Understanding these models is crucial for effectively integrating quality engineering practices.

2.2 SDLC and Role of Quality Engineer

SDLC stands for Software Development Life Cycle. It's a process that software developers follow to create and maintain software applications. SDLC models are different ways or approaches to managing these development processes. There are several popular SDLC models, each with its own steps and characteristics. Here are a few common ones.

2.3 Waterfall Methodology

The waterfall model follows a linear, sequential approach with distinct phases, including requirements gathering, design, implementation, testing, and maintenance. Each phase is completed before moving on to the next. While the waterfall model provides clear documentation and control, it lacks flexibility for changes and can result in late defect detection. Let's delve into the key stages of the Waterfall Model.

2.3.1 Requirements Phase

In this initial stage, project stakeholders gather and document all the software requirements. This involves understanding user needs, system functionalities, constraints, and expectations. Once the requirements are finalized and signed off, they serve as the foundation for the rest of the project.

2.3.2 System Design

During the system design phase, software architects and designers create a detailed blueprint of the system's architecture. This includes designing the overall structure, database schema, user interfaces, and interaction flows. The design phase ensures that all requirements are translated into a comprehensive technical plan.

2.3.3 Implementation (Coding) Phase

With the design in place, developers start writing code based on the design specifications. This phase involves translating the technical design into actual software components, modules, and features. The coding phase requires adherence to coding standards and best practices.

2.3.4 Testing Phase

Once the code is developed, the testing phase begins. Software testers evaluate the system's functionality, performance, and adherence to requirements. Testing includes unit testing (testing individual components), integration testing (testing how components work together), and system testing (testing the entire system).

2.3.5 Deployment Phase

After successful testing, the software is deployed to a production environment or made available to users. This phase involves installation, configuration, and setting up the software for use by end-users.

2.3.6 Maintenance Phase

The final phase involves ongoing maintenance and support of the software. This includes addressing any issues or defects that may arise after deployment, making necessary updates, and enhancing the software based on user feedback.

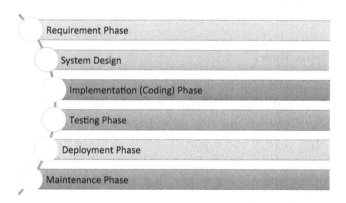

Waterfall methodology.

2.3.7 Advantages of Waterfall Methodology

- Clear Documentation: Each phase produces well-documented artifacts, aiding in project understanding and future maintenance.
- Predictability: The linear nature of the model allows for better project planning and resource allocation.
- Structured Approach: The sequential flow of phases ensures a systematic and organized development process.
- Well-Defined Milestones: Clear milestones mark the completion of each phase, providing a sense of progress.

2.3.8 Disadvantages of Waterfall Methodology

- Rigidity: The model is less adaptable to changes in requirements or unexpected developments.
- Late User Feedback: Users don't see the product until the end, potentially leading to misalignments with their expectations.
- Limited Iteration: Iteration is minimal, making it challenging to refine the product during development.
- Long Development Cycles: The linear approach can result in longer development cycles, delaying the delivery of the final product.

2.3.9 Conclusion

The Waterfall Model provides a structured and formalized approach to software.

2.4 The Spiral Model

The Spiral Model is a flexible and iterative software development methodology that combines elements of the Waterfall Model with iterative development and risk management. It was introduced by Barry Boehm in 1986 and is particularly well-suited for projects with uncertain or evolving requirements. The Spiral Model emphasizes continuous evaluation, adaptation, and risk mitigation throughout the development process. Let's explore the key features and stages of the Spiral Model.

Planning: The project's objectives, requirements, constraints, and risks are identified and defined. The initial plan outlines the scope, resources, and schedule of the project.

Risk Assessment: In this stage, potential risks and uncertainties are identified and analyzed. Risks can range from technical challenges to changing requirements or market shifts.

Engineering and Development: This phase involves creating the actual software product based on the initial plan and design. Iterative development begins, with each iteration producing a version of the software.

Evaluation: After each iteration, the software is evaluated. This includes testing, user feedback, and reviews to assess whether the software meets the requirements and quality expectations.

Planning the Next Iteration: Based on the evaluation, the project plan is reviewed and adjusted. The next iteration is planned, incorporating lessons learned and addressing identified issues.

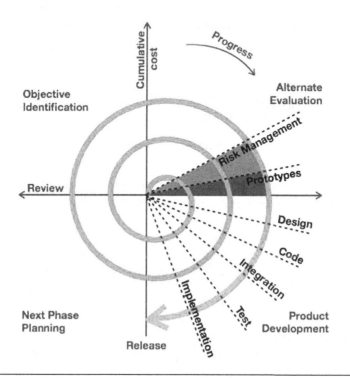

Spiral model.

2.4.1 Advantages of the Spiral Model

- Risk Management: The model's focus on risk assessment and mitigation helps identify and address potential issues early in the development process.
- Iterative Development: Iterative cycles allow for incremental improvements and adaptations based on user feedback and changing requirements.
- Flexibility: The model accommodates changes in requirements and project scope, making it suitable for dynamic or evolving projects.
- Continuous Improvement: Regular evaluations and adjustments promote continuous improvement in both the software product and the development process.

2.4.2 Disadvantages of the Spiral Model

- Complexity: The model's iterative nature can introduce complexity in project management and planning.
- Resource Intensive: Frequent iterations and evaluations require consistent resources and active stakeholder involvement.
- Documentation Challenges: Frequent iterations can lead to challenges in maintaining documentation and keeping all stakeholders informed.

2.4.3 When to Use the Spiral Model

The Spiral Model is suitable for projects that have: Evolving or uncertain requirements; high levels of technical complexity or innovation; a need for risk assessment and mitigation; a requirement for frequent user feedback; and budget and schedule flexibility.

2.4.4 Conclusion

The Spiral Model provides a structured yet flexible approach to software development, particularly well-suited for projects that involve uncertainty, evolving requirements, or high technical complexity. By iteratively planning, developing, evaluating, and adjusting, the model emphasizes risk management, continuous improvement, and adaptive development practices. The Spiral Model addresses the limitations of the Waterfall Model by enabling developers to navigate changing conditions and deliver software that aligns with user needs and project goals.

2.5 The Agile Model

Agile modeling is a dynamic and collaborative approach to software development that focuses on iterative development, flexibility, and effective communication among cross-functional teams. It is a key component of the broader Agile methodology, which prioritizes customer collaboration, incremental progress, and responding to change. Agile modeling seeks to create a balance between documentation and practical development, adapting to evolving requirements while maintaining a clear understanding of the software's design and functionality. Let's explore the principles and practices of Agile modeling.

Iterative and Incremental Development: Agile modeling emphasizes breaking the software development process into small, manageable iterations. Each iteration results in a working increment of the software that adds value to the product and can be demonstrated to stakeholders.

Continuous Feedback: Regular interactions with stakeholders, including users, customers, and team members, provide ongoing feedback that guides the development process. Feedback helps ensure that the software aligns with user needs and expectations.

Collaborative Approach: Agile modeling encourages collaboration among cross-functional teams, including developers, testers, designers, and business stakeholders. Open communication fosters shared understanding and informed decision-making.

Adaptive Documentation: Documentation is important, but Agile modeling values working software over excessive documentation. Documentation is kept concise and relevant, focusing on what is necessary to facilitate development and understanding.

Embracing Change: Agile modeling embraces change as a natural part of software development. Teams are prepared to adapt to changing requirements, priorities, and market conditions throughout the project.

CI: Agile modeling promotes CI, where code changes are frequently integrated into a shared repository. This practice helps identify integration issues early and ensures that the software remains stable.

Test-Driven Development (TDD): TDD is a core practice of Agile modeling, where tests are written before the actual code. This approach ensures that code is developed to meet specific requirements and that any changes are validated against tests.

User-Centric Design: Agile modeling places users at the center of the development process. Regular user feedback and usability testing ensure that the software is user-friendly and meets user needs.

Delivering Value: Each iteration of Agile modeling delivers a tangible increment of value to users. This allows for regular release of functional software, giving stakeholders a sense of progress.

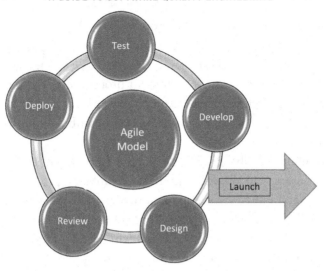

Agile methodology.

2.5.1 Advantages of Agile Modeling

- Customer Satisfaction: Regular feedback and user involvement ensure that the software meets customer expectations.
- Flexibility: Agile modeling adapts to changing requirements and market conditions.
- Reduced Risk: Frequent testing and validation mitigate the risk of delivering software that doesn't meet user needs.
- Collaborative Environment: Cross-functional teams collaborate closely, leading to better communication and understanding.

2.5.2 Disadvantages of Agile Modeling

- Lack of Predictability: Agile modeling's flexible nature can make it difficult to predict project outcomes with precision.
- Documentation Challenges: Minimal documentation can lead to difficulties in maintaining a clear record of decisions and design.

2.5.3 Conclusion

Agile modeling is a powerful approach that embodies the values of the Agile methodology, including adaptability, collaboration, and delivering value to users. By emphasizing iterative development, continuous feedback, and cross-functional teamwork, Agile modeling aims to create software that is not only functional and efficient but also aligns closely with user needs and expectations.

2.6 Iterative and Incremental Development

Iterative and Incremental Development is a software development approach that focuses on breaking down complex projects into manageable pieces, developing and refining them in successive cycles. This methodology emphasizes delivering working increments of the software at regular intervals, allowing for early feedback, continuous improvement, and flexibility in responding to changing requirements. Let's delve into the key principles and benefits of Iterative and Incremental Development.

The Iterative and Incremental Development Process:

2.6.1 Requirements Analysis

- Gather and prioritize requirements.
- Define the scope of the current iteration.

2.6.2 Design

- Design the solution for the current iteration's scope.
- Create mock-ups, prototypes, or wireframes.

2.6.3 Development

- Develop the software incrementally based on the design.
- Implement features, functionalities, and improvements.

2.6.4 Testing

- Test the developed features to identify defects and ensure functionality.
- Conduct unit, integration, and user acceptance testing (UAT).

2.6.5 Feedback and Review

- Demonstrate the working increment to stakeholders.
- Gather feedback and suggestions for improvements.

2.6.6 Adjustments and Refinement

- Incorporate feedback to refine the software increment.
- Make necessary changes based on user input.

2.6.7 Deployment

- Deploy the updated increment to the production environment.
- Ensure the new features integrate seamlessly.

2.6.8 Next Iteration Planning

- Plan the next iteration based on feedback, new requirements, and priorities.

2.6.9 Applying Iterative and Incremental Development

- Agile Methodology: Iterative and Incremental Development is a fundamental principle of Agile methodologies such as Scrum and Kanban.
- Complex Projects: It is effective for complex projects where requirements may evolve over time.
- Adaptive Development: It is well-suited for projects with changing needs, as it allows adjustments in each iteration.

2.6.9.1 Iteration In this approach, the development process is divided into multiple iterations, each of which includes a subset of features or functionalities. An iteration typically follows a complete development cycle from planning to deployment.

2.6.9.2 Increment Each iteration produces a working increment of the software that adds value and can be demonstrated to stakeholders. This increment might include new features, bug fixes, or improvements based on feedback.

2.6.10 Benefits of Iterative and Incremental Development

- Early Value Delivery: By delivering functional increments at the end of each iteration, users can start benefiting from the software sooner.

- User Feedback: Early releases enable users to provide feedback, helping the development team make necessary adjustments.
- Reduced Risk: Smaller iterations minimize the risk of large-scale project failure by allowing issues to be addressed early.
- Flexibility: Changing requirements can be accommodated in subsequent iterations, promoting adaptability.
- Continuous Improvement: The iterative nature promotes learning and refinement, resulting in an improved end product.
- Stakeholder Engagement: Regular demonstrations of working software keep stakeholders engaged and informed.

2.6.11 Conclusion

Iterative and Incremental Development is a powerful approach that fosters collaboration, delivers value incrementally, and enhances the quality of software. By focusing on frequent iterations, user feedback, and continuous improvement, this methodology helps developers create software that aligns closely with user needs, adapts to changes, and ultimately leads to a successful and user-centric end product.

2.7 V-Model

The V-Model, also known as the Verification and Validation Model, is a software development and testing methodology that emphasizes the relationship between development and testing phases. It is characterized by its structured and sequential approach, where each development phase corresponds to a testing phase. The model's name is derived from the visual representation of its process, resembling the letter "V." Let's explore the key concepts and stages of the V-Model.

Requirements Phase: In this initial stage, project stakeholders gather and document software requirements. The requirements are then used to create a detailed design specification.

System Design Phase: Based on the requirements, system architects and designers create a high-level design that outlines the overall system architecture and components.

High-Level Testing (Verification): In the V-Model, testing activities mirror development activities. After the system design phase, high-level testing is conducted to ensure that the design meets the requirements.

Detailed Design Phase: Detailed design specifications are developed based on the high-level design. These specifications outline the technical details of the software's components and interactions.

Low-Level Testing (Verification): Following the detailed design phase, low-level testing is performed to verify that the detailed design adheres to the high-level design and meets the requirements.

Implementation (Coding) Phase: Developers write the actual code based on the detailed design specifications. This phase involves translating the technical design into functioning software components.

Unit Testing (Verification): Unit testing is conducted to verify the correctness of individual software units or components. Each unit is tested in isolation to ensure it performs as intended.

Integration Phase: The individual software units or components are integrated to form the complete system. Integration testing ensures that the integrated parts work together seamlessly.

Integration Testing (Verification): Integration testing focuses on testing the interactions between integrated components to identify issues related to data flow, communication, and functionality.

System Testing (Validation): The fully integrated system is subjected to system testing, which validates its overall functionality, performance, and compliance with the specified requirements.

Validation and UAT: UAT is performed to ensure that the software meets user expectations and is ready for deployment.

V- Model

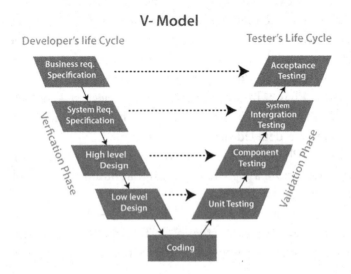

2.7.1 Advantages of the V-Model

- Structured Approach: The V-Model provides a clear and structured path from requirements to testing, ensuring comprehensive verification and validation.
- Traceability: The model emphasizes the traceability of requirements through each phase of development and testing.
- Early Detection of Defects: Testing activities run in parallel with development, allowing early detection and resolution of defects.
- Thorough Testing: The model promotes comprehensive testing, ensuring that all aspects of the software are validated and verified.

2.7.2 Disadvantages of the V-Model

- Rigidity: The V-Model can be less adaptable to changes in requirements compared to more flexible methodologies.
- Late User Involvement: Users may not provide feedback until the later testing phases, potentially leading to mismatches between expectations and deliverables.

2.7.3 Conclusion

The V-Model is a structured methodology that emphasizes the connection between development and testing activities. It ensures that software requirements are thoroughly verified and validated at each stage of the process. While it may not be as adaptive as some Agile methodologies, the V-Model is effective for projects with well-defined requirements and a need for rigorous testing and verification.

2.8 Rational Unified Process (RUP)

The RUP is a flexible and iterative software development framework that provides a structured approach to designing, implementing, and delivering software projects. RUP is based on industry best practices and incorporates principles from object-oriented design, iterative development, and process customization. It was developed by Rational Software (later acquired by IBM) and is designed to adapt to various project sizes and complexities. Let's delve into the key concepts and stages of the RUP.

Phases: RUP divides the software development lifecycle into a series of distinct phases, each focusing on specific activities and objectives.

Inception: During this initial phase, project stakeholders identify the project's scope, goals, and risks. A preliminary project plan is created, and a feasibility study is conducted to assess the project's viability.

Elaboration: This phase involves refining the project requirements, architecture, and design. It aims to mitigate major risks and create a comprehensive project plan for the development.

Construction: The construction phase focuses on developing the software incrementally based on the refined design. Regular iterations produce working increments that are tested, integrated, and refined.

Transition: The final phase involves preparing the software for deployment. This includes final testing, user training, documentation, and ensuring a smooth transition to the production environment.

Workflows: RUP organizes development activities into separate workflows, each corresponding to a key aspect of software development.

- Business Modeling: Focuses on understanding the business processes and requirements.
- Requirements: Focuses on gathering, documenting, and prioritizing system requirements.
- Analysis and Design: Involves creating detailed specifications and architectural designs.
- Implementation: Encompasses coding, testing, and integration of software components.
- Testing: Focuses on verifying and validating the software against requirements.
- Deployment: Focuses on deploying the software to users and maintaining its operation.

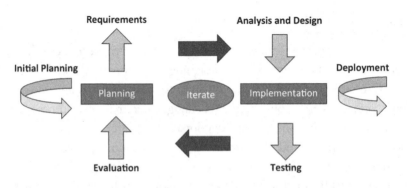

Iterative and incremental development.

Iterative and Incremental Development: RUP follows an iterative and incremental development approach. Each phase and workflow include multiple iterations that produce tangible increments of the software. This allows for early user feedback, continuous improvement, and adaptability to changing requirements.

Architecture-Centric Approach: RUP places a strong emphasis on architectural design. Architectural decisions are made early in the project and guide subsequent development activities, ensuring a coherent and well-designed system.

Customization and Tailoring: RUP is highly customizable, allowing development teams to tailor the process to their specific needs, project size, and organizational context.

Artifact-Centric: RUP encourages the creation of well-documented artifacts, including models, diagrams, and documentation. These artifacts ensure clear communication and understanding among team members and stakeholders.

2.8.1 Advantages of RUP

- Structured Approach: RUP provides a well-defined framework that guides the entire software development lifecycle.
- Adaptability: Its iterative and incremental nature allows for flexibility and responsiveness to changes.
- Early Risk Mitigation: RUP's emphasis on risk assessment and mitigation helps address potential issues early in the project.
- Comprehensive Documentation: The framework encourages the creation of artifacts that aid communication and knowledge sharing.

2.8.2 Disadvantages of RUP

- Complexity: The comprehensive nature of RUP can make it challenging to implement and manage smaller projects.
- Resource Intensive: RUP requires skilled personnel and resources for effective implementation.

2.8.3 Conclusion

The RUP is a comprehensive software development framework that emphasizes iterative development, architectural design, and adaptability. By breaking the development process into distinct phases, workflows, and iterations, RUP provides a structured yet flexible approach to software development that can be customized to suit different project sizes and complexities.

2.9 The DevOps Model

The DevOps model is a collaborative and cultural approach to software development and IT operations that aims to streamline the software delivery process, enhance collaboration, and improve the quality and speed of software releases. DevOps breaks down traditional silos between development and operations teams, encouraging shared responsibilities and continuous communication. It combines development (Dev) and operations (Ops) practices to achieve faster delivery of high-quality software. Let's delve into the key principles and practices of the DevOps model.

Collaboration and Communication: DevOps emphasizes breaking down the barriers between development and operations teams. Collaboration and communication are prioritized to ensure shared understanding, cooperation, and alignment of goals.

Automation: Automation is a cornerstone of DevOps. It involves automating various processes, such as building, testing, deployment, and monitoring, to reduce manual errors and accelerate the software delivery pipeline.

Continuous Integration (CI): CI involves integrating code changes from multiple developers into a shared repository multiple times a day. Automated testing and validation are performed to ensure that new code changes do not introduce defects.

Continuous Delivery (CD): CD extends CI by automating the deployment process. It ensures that code changes can be reliably and rapidly deployed to production or staging environments, enabling frequent and reliable releases.

Infrastructure as Code (IaC): IaC treats infrastructure setup and configuration as code, allowing infrastructure to be provisioned, managed, and versioned in a consistent and automated manner.

Monitoring and Feedback: Continuous monitoring of applications and infrastructure helps identify issues early. Feedback loops provide insights into the software's performance, user experience, and potential improvements.

Microservices Architecture: DevOps often pairs with microservices architecture, where applications are broken down into smaller, independently deployable services. This enables flexibility, scalability, and easier maintenance.

Security Integration: Security is integrated throughout the software development lifecycle. DevOps teams collaborate to ensure that security measures are built into every stage of development and deployment.

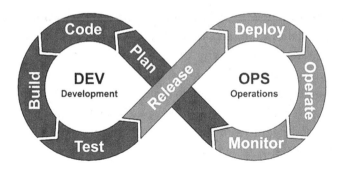

DevOps model.

2.9.1 Benefits of the DevOps Model

- Faster Time-to-Market: Automation and CD enable quicker releases, allowing organizations to respond rapidly to market demands.
- Improved Collaboration: Close collaboration between teams leads to reduced misunderstandings, improved communication, and shared responsibility.
- Enhanced Quality: Automation and continuous testing lead to more reliable and consistent software releases with fewer defects.

- Efficiency and Scalability: Automation allows efficient management of infrastructure and scalability to handle varying workloads.
- Reduced Risk: Frequent testing, monitoring, and early feedback reduce the risk of issues reaching production.

2.9.2 Challenges of the DevOps Model

- Cultural Shift: Transitioning to DevOps requires a cultural shift and a mindset change among team members.
- Complexity: Implementing automation and continuous practices can introduce complexity to the development process.
- Learning Curve: Teams need to acquire new skills related to automation, infrastructure management, and collaborative practices.

2.9.3 Conclusion

The DevOps model revolutionizes software development by fostering collaboration, automation, and continuous improvement. By integrating development and operations practices, DevOps accelerates software delivery, enhances quality, and enables organizations to respond swiftly to changing requirements and market conditions. It's a transformative approach that aligns technology, processes, and people to drive innovation and deliver value to users and stakeholders.

2.10 Quality Assurance (QA) in SDLC

QA activities ensure that software products and processes meet defined quality standards. QA plays a crucial role in each phase of the SDLC to prevent defects, verify compliance, and ensure customer satisfaction.

- Requirements Phase: Quality engineering begins with requirements engineering, where quality engineers collaborate with stakeholders to ensure clear, complete, and testable requirements. They review requirements for clarity, consistency, and feasibility, identifying potential risks and suggesting improvements.

- Design Phase: In the design phase, quality engineers participate in design reviews to assess adherence to quality standards and verify that design choices align with requirements. They evaluate design documents, identify potential quality risks, and recommend appropriate design patterns and best practices.
- Implementation Phase: Quality engineers collaborate with developers to ensure coding standards, best practices, and quality guidelines are followed. They perform code reviews, static analysis, and pair programming to identify code defects, improve maintainability, and promote quality-conscious coding.
- Testing Phase: Quality engineers play a central role in testing activities. They develop test strategies, design test cases, execute tests, and analyze test results. They verify functional correctness, conduct performance and security testing, and ensure the software meets quality expectations.
- Deployment and Maintenance Phase: Quality engineering continues even after software deployment. Quality engineers monitor production systems, collect and analyze user feedback, and address reported defects promptly. They also collaborate with operations teams to ensure system stability and performance.

"To overcome the challenges and elevate software quality in architecture design, the proposed survey-based approach presents a holistic framework. By collecting data from diverse sources, such as stakeholders, end-users, subject matter experts, and historical project data, architects gain invaluable insights into the essential software quality attributes. The integration of superlative attributes, such as Performance, Dependability, and Safety concerns, empowers architects to make informed decisions during the design process" [2].

2.11 Role of Quality Engineer in SDLC

The role of a quality engineer is crucial to maintaining and improving software quality throughout the SDLC. A quality engineer collaborates with cross-functional teams, drives quality initiatives, and applies engineering principles to ensure high-quality software deliverables.

- Requirements Engineer: Quality engineers participate in requirements engineering activities, ensuring that requirements are clear, measurable, and testable. They collaborate with stakeholders to elicit requirements and validate them for quality attributes.
- Design Reviewer: Quality engineers contribute to design reviews, verifying that designs align with quality standards and addressing potential risks. They assess design choices, identify design flaws, and suggest improvements to enhance software quality.
- Test Engineer: Quality engineers are responsible for designing test strategies, creating test plans, and executing test cases. They perform various types of testing, such as functional, integration, performance, and security testing, to ensure software quality.
- Automation Engineer: Quality engineers develop and maintain test automation frameworks, scripts, and tools to accelerate testing processes and improve efficiency. They identify suitable test cases for automation and implement robust automation practices.

2.12 Case Study

CASE STUDY: IMPLEMENTING QUALITY ENGINEERING IN AN AGILE SDLC

In this case study, we explore how a software development team successfully integrated quality engineering practice into an agile SDLC.

Example: United Systems Group adopted an agile approach, implementing Scrum methodology. The quality engineer actively participated in sprint planning, providing input on quality goals, test coverage, and the testability of user stories.

During development, the quality engineer collaborated closely with developers, performing code reviews, and suggesting improvements for code quality and maintainability. The quality engineer also created a comprehensive suite of automated tests covering functional, integration, and regression scenarios.

Throughout the sprint, the quality engineer continuously executed tests, reported defects, and provided immediate feedback to the development team. This collaborative effort ensured early defect detection, prompt resolution, and improved software quality.

Practical Exercise:

- Reflect on your organization's current SDLC model and the role of quality engineering within it. Consider the following exercises:
- Analyze your SDLC model and identify its strengths and weaknesses in terms of software quality.
- Assess the level of collaboration between quality engineers and other stakeholders in each phase of the SDLC.
- Identify potential areas for improvement in integrating quality engineering practices effectively.
- Evaluate the roles and responsibilities of quality engineers in your organization and compare them to industry best practices.
- Develop a roadmap for enhancing the role of quality engineering in your organization's SDLC, considering specific action items and timelines.

By completing these exercises, you can gain insights into the current state of quality engineering in your organization and identify opportunities for improvement in integrating quality practices into your SDLC model.

In the next chapter, we will dive deeper into software testing principles and techniques, providing a comprehensive understanding of how quality engineers ensure software quality through effective testing strategies.

Note: This chapter provides a comprehensive overview of SDLC models and the role of quality engineering within them. Case studies, examples, and practical exercises are included to reinforce the concepts and encourage reflection. Subsequent chapters will focus on specific aspects of quality engineering within the SDLC to provide a deeper understanding of software quality practices.

3

SOFTWARE TESTING PRINCIPLES AND TECHNIQUES

Software testing is a crucial aspect of ensuring high-quality software products. In this chapter, we will explore the fundamental principles and techniques of software testing used by quality engineers to verify and validate software functionality, performance, and security.

3.1 Testing Objectives and Goals

Software testing aims to uncover defects and ensure that the software meets quality expectations. Testing objectives and goals provide a clear direction for quality engineers and guide their efforts in achieving desired outcomes.

3.1.1 Defect Detection

The primary objective of testing is to detect defects and ensure they are addressed before software is released to users. Quality engineers design tests to identify failures and deviations from expected behavior.

3.1.2 Validation and Verification

Testing validates that the software meets the specified requirements and verifies that it behaves as expected. It ensures that the software performs its intended functions accurately and reliably.

3.1.3 Quality Assessment

Testing provides insights into the quality of the software, helping stakeholders assess its strengths, weaknesses, and fitness for purpose.

DOI: 10.1201/9781032702049-3

Quality engineers evaluate various quality attributes, such as functionality, reliability, performance, and security.

3.1.4 Risk Mitigation

Testing helps mitigate risks associated with software defects. By identifying and addressing defects early, quality engineers minimize the likelihood of failures, financial losses, and reputational damage.

CASE STUDY: EFFECTIVE TESTING OBJECTIVES AT OMEGA SYSTEMS INC.

In this case study, we examine how **Omega Systems Inc.** established clear testing objectives and successfully achieved them.

Example: Omega Systems Inc. identified the primary testing objective as defect prevention. They aimed to shift their testing efforts leftward in the SDLC to detect defects early, reducing rework, and enhancing software quality. The quality engineers worked closely with the development team to promote a culture of quality consciousness. To validate and verify the software, **Omega Systems Inc.** set specific testing goals for each release. These goals included achieving a certain level of code coverage, uncovering critical defects, and ensuring adherence to quality standards. The testing efforts were aligned with these goals, resulting in improved software reliability and customer satisfaction.

Practical Exercise:

- Define specific testing objectives and goals for a software project in your organization. Consider the following questions:
- What is the primary objective of testing for this project?
- Are there any specific quality attributes or functional requirements that need to be validated and verified?
- What risks are associated with the project, and how can testing mitigate them?
- How can testing contribute to the overall quality assessment of the software?

> • How do the testing objectives align with the organization's broader quality goals and customer expectations?

By defining clear testing objectives and goals, you can provide a sense of direction to the testing efforts and ensure alignment with broader quality objectives.

3.2 Level of Software Testing

Software testing can be performed at various levels, targeting different aspects of the software system. Understanding these levels helps quality engineers design a comprehensive testing approach.

3.2.1 Unit Testing

Unit testing focuses on testing individual components or units of the software in isolation. It verifies the correctness of code at the lowest level and helps identify defects early in the development process.

3.2.2 Integration Testing

Integration testing verifies the interaction and communication between different units or components of the software. It ensures that the integrated system functions as expected and that the units work together seamlessly.

3.2.3 System Testing

System testing examines the behavior of the entire software system as a whole. It validates that the system meets functional and non-functional requirements and ensures proper integration with external components and interfaces.

3.2.4 Acceptance Testing

Acceptance testing is performed to validate whether the software meets the requirements and expectations of the end-users or stakeholders. It assesses the software's fitness for purpose and determines if it is ready for deployment.

CASE STUDY: EFFECTIVE LEVEL-WISE TESTING

In this case study, we explore how **Omega Systems Inc.** implemented a level-wise testing approach to achieve comprehensive testing coverage.

Example: Omega Systems Inc. adopted a level-wise testing strategy, starting with unit testing by developers during development. Once units were integrated, integration testing was performed to ensure smooth interaction between components.

Following integration, system testing was conducted by quality engineers to validate the system's behavior and verify its compliance with requirements. Finally, acceptance testing involved end-users or stakeholders to ensure the software met their needs.

This level-wise approach enabled **Omega Systems Inc.** to detect defects at different levels of the system, resulting in improved software reliability and reduced post-deployment issues.

Practical Exercise:

- Design a level-wise testing strategy for a software project in your organization.

Consider the following aspects:

- Identify the appropriate levels of testing based on the complexity and criticality of the software system.
- Determine the testing techniques and tools suitable for each level of testing.
- Define the entry and exit criteria for transitioning between different levels of testing.
- Identify the resources and skills required for executing each level of testing effectively.
- Consider how the level-wise testing approach aligns with the overall project timeline and resource allocation.

By designing a level-wise testing strategy, you can ensure comprehensive testing coverage and identify defects at different levels of the software system.

3.3 Testing Techniques and Strategies

Testing techniques and strategies provide a structured approach to test design and execution. They help quality engineers optimize their testing efforts and improve the effectiveness of defect detection.

3.3.1 Black Box Testing

Black box testing focuses on validating the software's external behavior without considering its internal structure or implementation details. Test cases are designed based on functional requirements, and inputs and expected outputs are analyzed.

3.3.2 White Box Testing

White box testing, also known as structural testing, examines the internal structure of the software. It verifies the correctness of code, checks the flow of control, and analyzes the execution paths. Techniques such as statement coverage, branch coverage, and path coverage are used.

3.3.3 Gray Box Testing

Gray box testing combines elements of black box and white box testing. Testers have partial knowledge of the internal structure, allowing them to design tests that cover specific areas of interest. It combines the advantages of both techniques.

3.3.4 Regression Testing

Regression testing ensures that changes or additions to the software do not introduce new defects or disrupt existing functionality. It retests previously tested features and verifies that the software still behaves as intended after modifications.

CASE STUDY: EFFECTIVE TESTING TECHNIQUES

In this case study, we examine how **Vertex Services Ltd** applied effective testing techniques to improve the quality of their software.

Example: Vertex Services Ltd utilized a combination of black box and white box testing techniques. Black box testing was used to verify functional requirements, ensuring that the software performed the intended operations correctly. White box testing techniques, such as code coverage analysis and boundary value analysis, were employed to assess code quality, control flow, and data handling. This helped identify defects related to code logic and uncover potential vulnerabilities. The integration of both techniques enabled **Vertex Services Ltd** to achieve comprehensive test coverage and uncover defects at different levels of the software system.

Practical Exercise:

- Select a software project in your organization and choose appropriate testing techniques for effective defect detection. Consider the following:
- Identify the types of defects that are more likely to occur in the software system.
- Determine the level of access and knowledge available to testers regarding the software's internal structure.
- Evaluate the impact of changes or additions to the software on existing functionality.
- Consider the resources, tools, and expertise required to implement the selected testing techniques effectively.
- Define a strategy for combining different testing techniques to achieve comprehensive test coverage.

By selecting appropriate testing techniques and strategies, you can improve the efficiency and effectiveness of defect detection in your software projects.

3.4 Test Case Design and Execution

Test case design and execution form the core of software testing activities. Quality engineers create test cases based on requirements, execute them, and analyze the results to ensure thorough coverage and defect detection.

3.4.1 Test Case Design Techniques

Various techniques can be used to design effective test cases, including equivalence partitioning, boundary value analysis, decision table testing, state transition testing, and case-based testing. These techniques help identify test conditions and inputs for effective test case creation. Let's explore some common test case design techniques.

- Equivalence Partitioning: This technique divides input values into classes or partitions that are expected to behave similarly. Test cases are then designed to cover representative values from each partition. For example, if an input field accepts values from 1 to 100, test cases might include values like 1, 50, and 100.
- Boundary Value Analysis: Boundary value analysis focuses on values at the edges of equivalence partitions. Test cases are designed to test both the valid and invalid boundary values. For example, if a password field requires 8 to 16 characters, test cases might include passwords with exactly 8, 16, and 9 characters.
- Decision Table Testing: Decision tables map combinations of conditions and their corresponding actions or outcomes. Test cases are designed to cover various combinations of conditions and validate the expected outcomes. This technique is useful for testing business rules and complex decision-making processes.
- State Transition Testing: This technique is employed when the software system has different states and transitions between them. Test cases are designed to cover various state transitions and ensure that the software behaves correctly during these transitions.

- Pairwise Testing (Combinatorial Testing): Pairwise testing selects a combination of input values that test all possible pairs of input values. It aims to minimize the number of test cases while maximizing the coverage of interactions between input variables.

- Use Case Testing: Use case testing involves designing test cases based on user scenarios or interactions with the software. It ensures that the software behaves as intended in real-world usage scenarios.

- Error Guessing: Error guessing relies on the tester's experience and intuition to anticipate potential defects and design test cases to expose those defects. This technique is particularly useful when there is limited documentation or time for formal test design.

- Random Testing: Random testing involves generating random inputs and executing test cases without specific scenarios. It can help identify unexpected defects that might not be uncovered through other techniques.

- Exploratory Testing: Exploratory testing is a dynamic approach where testers explore software applications while testing. Test cases are created on the fly based on the tester's intuition and observations, allowing for uncovering defects through ad-hoc exploration.

- Regression Testing: Regression testing involves designing test cases to verify that new code changes do not introduce defects or regressions in existing functionality. It ensures that the previous working features continue to work as expected.

3.5 Software Testing Principles

Software testing principles are fundamental guidelines that provide a foundation for effective and efficient testing practices. These principles help testing teams ensure that software applications meet quality standards, perform as expected, and are free from defects. By adhering to these principles, testing professionals can contribute to the overall success of the software development process. Let's explore some key software testing principles.

- Exhaustive Testing is Impossible: It is practically impossible to test all possible scenarios, inputs, and combinations. Instead, testing efforts should focus on critical and high-risk areas while using techniques that provide maximum coverage within time and resource constraints.
- Testing Reveals Defects: The primary purpose of testing is to identify defects or deviations from expected behavior. Successful testing exposes defects, helping developers address them before the software is released.
- Early Testing: Testing activities should begin as early as possible in the software development lifecycle. Identifying defects early minimizes their impact and reduces the cost of fixing them.
- Defect Clustering: A small number of modules or components often contain a majority of defects. Focusing testing efforts on these critical areas can yield significant defect detection.

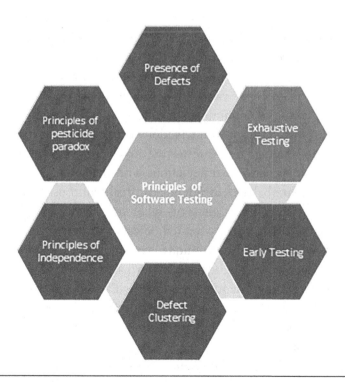

Principles of software testing.

Equivalence Partitioning: This technique divides input values into classes or partitions that are expected to behave similarly. Test cases are then designed to cover representative values from each partition. For example, if an input field accepts values from 1 to 100, test cases might include values like 1, 50, and 100.

Boundary Value Analysis: Boundary value analysis focuses on values at the edges of equivalence partitions. Test cases are designed to test both the valid and invalid boundary values. For example, if a password field requires 8 to 16 characters, test cases might include passwords with exactly 8, 16, and 9 characters.

Decision Table Testing: Decision tables map combinations of conditions and their corresponding actions or outcomes. Test cases are designed to cover various combinations of conditions and validate the expected outcomes. This technique is useful for testing business rules and complex decision-making processes.

State Transition Testing: This technique is employed when the software system has different states and transitions between them. Test cases are designed to cover various state transitions and ensure that the software behaves correctly during these transitions.

Pairwise Testing (Combinatorial Testing): Pairwise testing selects a combination of input values that test all possible pairs of input values. It aims to minimize the number of test cases while maximizing the coverage of interactions between input variables.

Use Case Testing: Use case testing involves designing test cases based on user scenarios or interactions with the software. It ensures that the software behaves as intended in real-world usage scenarios.

Error Guessing: Error guessing relies on the tester's experience and intuition to anticipate potential defects and design test cases to expose those defects. This technique is particularly useful when there is limited documentation or time for formal test design.

Random Testing: Random testing involves generating random inputs and executing test cases without specific scenarios. It can help identify unexpected defects that might not be uncovered through other techniques.

Exploratory Testing: Exploratory testing is a dynamic approach where testers explore software applications while testing. Test cases are created on the fly based on the tester's intuition and observations, allowing for uncovering defects through ad-hoc exploration.

Regression Testing: Regression testing involves designing test cases to verify that new code changes do not introduce defects or regressions in existing functionality. It ensures that the previous working features continue to work as expected.

"As a process (the process of identifying stakeholders, eliciting requirements, compiling them, etc.), a specification must meet two conditions, which are as follows:

Completeness: The specification must capture all the relevant requirements of the product.

Minimality: The specification must capture nothing but the relevant requirements of the product" [3].

3.5.1 Test Case Execution

Test case execution involves running the designed test cases and observing the actual behavior of the software. Quality engineers meticulously execute test cases, record the results, and report any discrepancies or failures.

3.5.2 Test Case Management

Test case management encompasses organizing, prioritizing, and tracking test cases throughout the testing process. Test case management tools can be used to streamline this process, ensuring efficient test case execution and traceability.

3.6 Advantages and Disadvantages of Software Testing

- Defect Detection: Testing helps identify defects and issues in the software, allowing developers to address them before the software is released to users.
- Quality Improvement: Testing improves the overall quality of the software by ensuring that it meets functional and performance requirements.
- User Satisfaction: Thorough testing results in a more stable and reliable software product, leading to higher user satisfaction and trust.

- Risk Mitigation: Testing helps identify and mitigate risks associated with software failures or defects, reducing the chances of critical issues in production.
- Cost Savings: Detecting and fixing defects early in the development lifecycle is more cost-effective than addressing them after deployment.
- Enhanced Security: Security testing helps identify vulnerabilities and weaknesses in the software, minimizing the risk of security breaches.
- Effective Decision Making: Testing provides data and insights that assist stakeholders in making informed decisions about the software's readiness for deployment.
- Compliance and Standards: Testing ensures that the software adheres to industry standards, regulatory requirements, and user expectations.

Disadvantages of Software Testing:

- Time-Consuming: Testing can extend the development timeline, especially if comprehensive and thorough testing is performed.
- Resource Intensive: Effective testing requires skilled testers, test environments, and appropriate testing tools, which can strain resources.
- Possibility of Incomplete Testing: It is impossible to test all scenarios exhaustively, leaving a chance that some defects may go unnoticed.
- False Sense of Security: Passing all tests does not guarantee that the software is completely free of defects or issues.
- Complexity: Testing complex systems with multiple interactions and dependencies can be challenging and may require specialized techniques.
- Late Detection: If testing is deferred until late in the development process, defects found may require significant rework, causing delays.
- Lack of Real-World Simulation: Testing environments might not fully simulate real-world conditions, leading to unanticipated issues in production.

- Changing Requirements: Frequent changes in requirements or scope can affect the effectiveness of previously designed tests.

CASE STUDY: EFFECTIVE TEST CASE DESIGN AND EXECUTION

In this case study, we explore how Prime Tech Solutions implemented effective test case design and execution practices to enhance their software testing efforts.

Example: Prime Tech Solutions employed equivalence partitioning and boundary value analysis techniques to design test cases. By categorizing inputs into valid and invalid equivalence classes and considering boundary values, they ensured comprehensive coverage. During test case execution, Prime Tech Solutions maintained detailed test logs, documenting the steps performed, expected results, and actual results. This facilitated efficient defect reporting and helped with root cause analysis.

Practical Exercise:

- Design and execute test cases for a specific software feature or module in your organization. Consider the following steps:
- Identify the requirements and functional specifications for the chosen feature or module.
- Apply appropriate test case design techniques, such as equivalence partitioning or boundary value analysis, to identify relevant test conditions and inputs.
- Create test cases with clear steps, expected results, and any necessary test data or preconditions.
- Execute the test cases systematically, recording the actual results and any observed discrepancies.
- Analyze the test results, categorize failures, and report defects as necessary.

By practicing test case design and execution, you can ensure comprehensive coverage, effective defect detection, and improved software quality.

In the next chapter, we will explore software quality metrics and measurement techniques, providing insights into how quality engineers evaluate and quantify software quality throughout the testing process.

Note: This chapter focuses on software testing principles and techniques, providing detailed explanations, case studies, examples, and practical exercises. The inclusion of these elements aims to enhance understanding and enable the practical application of the concepts discussed. Subsequent chapters will delve deeper into specific aspects of software quality engineering to provide a comprehensive understanding of the field.

4

TEST PLANNING AND MANAGEMENT

4.1 Test Planning Process

The test planning process is a crucial step in software development, encompassing the definition of the overall approach and scope of testing activities for a project. It involves identifying objectives, allocating resources, setting timelines, and outlining dependencies for testing while also establishing test deliverables.

4.1.1 Test Planning Activities

The process of test planning involves several key activities to ensure a well-structured and comprehensive testing approach. It begins with understanding project requirements, which helps in defining clear test objectives and identifying essential test deliverables. Environmental, determining the appropriate test environment and infrastructure requirements is crucial for successful testing. Test planning defines the scope, objectives, resources, schedules, and approach for testing. This process helps testing teams align their efforts with project goals and ensure efficient and effective testing. Let's explore the key steps in the test planning process.

- Understand Requirements and Objectives: The first step is to thoroughly understand the software requirements, user expectations, and project objectives. This forms the foundation for defining testing goals and strategies.
- Define Testing Scope: Clearly define the scope of testing by identifying the features, functionalities, and areas of the

DOI: 10.1201/9781032702049-4

software that need to be tested. This ensures that testing efforts are focused on the most critical aspects of the software.

- Set Testing Goals and Objectives: Based on the project's requirements and user needs, establish specific testing goals and objectives. These goals provide a clear direction for the testing effort and guide the team's activities.

- Select Testing Techniques and Tools: Choose appropriate testing techniques, methodologies, and tools that align with the project's characteristics and objectives. This includes deciding whether to perform manual testing, automated testing, or a combination of both.

- Allocate Resources: Determine the human and technical resources required for testing. Allocate roles and responsibilities among team members, including testers, test managers, and any other stakeholders involved in the testing process.

- Create Test Schedule: Develop a timeline that outlines when testing activities will occur, including testing phases, iterations, and milestones. The schedule should account for factors such as development timelines and project dependencies.

- Identify Test Environments: Specify the environments in which testing will be conducted, such as testing environments, staging environments, and production-like environments. Ensure that these environments closely simulate real-world conditions.

- Design Test Cases and Scenarios: Develop detailed test cases and testing scenarios based on the defined scope and objectives. These test cases outline the steps, inputs, expected outcomes, and conditions for each test.

- Establish Entry and Exit Criteria: Set entry criteria that define when testing can begin and exit criteria that specify when testing can be concluded. These criteria ensure that the software is ready for testing and release.

- Determine Bug Tracking and Reporting: Define procedures for reporting and tracking defects discovered during testing. Establish guidelines for documenting defects, severity levels, and the process for resolving issues.

- Review and Approve the Test Plan: Collaborate with stakeholders, including development teams and project managers, to review and approve the test plan. Incorporate feedback and ensure alignment with project goals.
- Monitor and Update the Plan: Regularly monitor the progress of testing activities against the plan. Update the plan as necessary to accommodate changes in requirements, scope, or project timelines.
- "I find identifying and documenting these open issues and questions to be among the most useful aspects of the planning exercise. Writing the plan forces me to think through the entire test effort — tools, processes, people, and technology — and to confront issues that I might otherwise miss" [4].

4.1.2 Test Planning Documentation

Effective test planning relies on well-documented strategies and guidelines. Key documents include the Test Plan, which outlines the overall test strategy, scope, and approach; the Test Schedule, which details testing timelines and milestones; and the Test Environment Setup document, which specifies the necessary infrastructure and test environment requirements. These documents serve as a roadmap for testing activities and ensure that all stakeholders are aligned on the testing process. It provides a clear reference point for testers, developers, project managers, and other team members involved in the testing effort. Let's explore the key components of test planning documentation.

- Introduction: The introduction section provides an overview of the test plan, including the purpose, scope, and objectives of testing. It outlines the software application to be tested, its key features, and the expected outcomes of testing.
- Test Strategy: The test strategy outlines the overall approach and methodologies that will be used for testing. It defines the types of testing to be performed (e.g., functional, perform-ance, security), the testing techniques, and the criteria for choosing between manual and automated testing.

- Scope and Objectives: This section defines the scope of testing by specifying the features, functionalities, and components that will be tested. It also outlines the objectives of testing, including quality goals, risk mitigation, and user satisfaction.
- Testing Schedule: The testing schedule outlines the timeline for testing activities, including testing phases, iterations, and milestones. It aligns with the project timeline and considers development cycles and release dates.
- Test Environment: This section describes the testing environments that will be used, including hardware, software, and network configurations. It ensures that the testing environments closely simulate the production environment.
- Testing Resources: The testing resources section outlines the roles and responsibilities of team members involved in testing, such as testers, test managers, developers, and stakeholders. It also identifies the required tools, software, and hardware resources.
- Test Cases and Scenarios: Detailed test cases and scenarios are provided in this section. Each test case includes step-by-step instructions, inputs, expected outcomes, and conditions for execution. It ensures that testing activities are well-documented and organized.
- Entry and Exit Criteria: Entry criteria specify the conditions that must be met for testing to begin, such as the completion of development. Exit criteria define the conditions that signal the end of testing, such as a predefined defect threshold or successful completion of test cases.
- Bug Tracking and Reporting: This section outlines the procedures for reporting and tracking defects, including defect categories, severity levels, and the process for resolution. It ensures that defects are effectively managed and communicated.
- Risks and Mitigation Strategies: Identify potential risks associated with testing, such as time constraints, incomplete requirements, or resource limitations. Provide strategies for mitigating these risks and minimizing their impact on testing.

- Sign-Off and Approval: The sign-off and approval section defines the process for reviewing, revising, and approving the test plan. It outlines the roles of stakeholders, project managers, and team members in approving the plan.

4.1.3 Conclusion

Summarize the key points of the test plan, reiterate its importance, and emphasize its role in ensuring the quality and reliability of the software application.

CASE STUDY: EFFECTIVE TEST PLANNING AT ELITE TECH INDUSTRIES

In this case study, we examine how Elite Tech Industries implemented an effective test planning process to ensure thorough testing of their software.

Example: Elite Tech Industries adopted a structured approach to test planning, starting with an in-depth analysis of project requirements to identify key quality objectives. Based on this analysis, they defined the scope of testing, focusing on the features and functionalities that required particular attention.

At Elite Tech Industries, the test planning process involved close collaboration between quality engineers, project managers, and stakeholders. The Test Plan served as a roadmap, documenting the test strategy, objectives, entry and exit criteria, and test deliverables. This provided clear direction for testing efforts, ensuring alignment with project goals.

Practical Exercise:

- Let's design a test planning process for a software project in your organization.

  Follow these steps:
- Gather and analyze project requirements to understand the scope and objectives of testing.

- Define the test objectives and identify key quality attributes to focus on during testing.
- Identify the necessary test deliverables, such as the Test Plan, Test Schedule, and Test Environment Setup document.
- Determine the test environment and infrastructure requirements, including hardware, software, and network configurations.
- Collaborate with project stakeholders to validate the test planning process and ensure alignment with project goals.

By adhering to a structured test planning process, you can ensure comprehensive test coverage, effective resource utilization, and the successful achievement of project quality objectives.

4.2 Test Strategy and Approach

The test strategy and approach define how testing will be conducted to achieve the desired quality objectives. It outlines the testing techniques, levels of testing, and types of testing to be employed during the project.

4.2.1 Test Levels and Types

A well-crafted test strategy clearly defines the levels and types of testing that will be executed. This includes unit testing, integration testing, system testing, and acceptance testing at different levels, as well as functional testing, performance testing, security testing, and usability testing as various types of testing. In the last chapter, we learned about test levels. In this chapter, let's learn more about testing types.

- Functional Testing: Functional testing verifies that the software functions according to its requirements. It involves testing individual functions, features, and user interactions to ensure they perform as expected.

- Non-Functional Testing: Non-functional testing focuses on aspects beyond functionality, such as performance, security, usability, and compatibility. This includes testing how the software handles stress, security vulnerabilities, and user experience.
- Regression Testing: Regression testing ensures that new code changes do not introduce defects or negatively impact existing functionality. It involves retesting existing features to catch regressions.
- Security Testing: Security testing identifies vulnerabilities and weaknesses in the software that could lead to security breaches. It ensures that the software can withstand various types of attacks.
- Usability Testing: Usability testing evaluates the software's user-friendliness, ease of use, and overall user experience. It ensures that the software is intuitive and meets user expectations.
- Compatibility Testing: Compatibility testing checks how the software functions across different devices, browsers, operating systems, and network environments. It ensures consistent performance on various platforms.
- Exploratory Testing: Exploratory testing involves testers exploring software and using their creativity to uncover defects. It relies on testers' intuition and experience to identify unexpected issues.
- Performance Testing: Performance testing assesses the software's responsiveness, scalability, and stability under varying load conditions. It includes load testing, stress testing, and performance profiling. Performance testing encompasses a diverse range of techniques that evaluate a software system's responsiveness, scalability, stability, and resource utilization. Unlike functional testing, which focuses on the correctness of software behavior, performance testing addresses how well an application can handle real-world usage scenarios. By subjecting applications to controlled loads and stress levels, performance testing identifies potential bottlenecks, uncovers system limitations, and offers a clear understanding of how the software behaves in production-like environments.

4.2.1.1 Performance Testing Methodologies

- Load Testing: Load testing involves subjecting a software system to varying levels of user load to evaluate its response times, resource utilization, and overall performance under different usage scenarios. This methodology helps identify performance bottlenecks, such as slow response times or server crashes, that might emerge as user traffic increases.

- Stress Testing: Stress testing takes performance evaluation a step further by pushing the application to its limits or beyond. By applying extreme loads, stress testing reveals how the system behaves when resources are scarce, database connections are saturated, or hardware components are under strain. This methodology uncovers potential failure points and helps assess system recovery mechanisms.

- Scalability Testing: Scalability testing aims to determine how well a software system can handle increased loads by adding more resources, such as servers or virtual machines. It assesses whether the application's performance scales linearly with added resources or if diminishing returns or bottlenecks emerge. This methodology is crucial for planning capacity upgrades.

- Endurance Testing: Endurance testing, also known as soak testing, involves subjecting an application to a sustained load for an extended period. This methodology helps uncover memory leaks, resource depletion, and other performance degradation issues that might only surface after prolonged usage.

- Spike Testing: Spike testing examines the application's response to sudden and extreme increases in user load. It simulates scenarios where user traffic spikes unexpectedly, as might occur during a product launch or breaking news event. This methodology assesses how well the system handles rapid fluctuations in demand.

- Volume Testing: Volume testing focuses on evaluating the system's performance when dealing with large volumes of data. It helps identify database performance issues, data handling bottlenecks, and potential data corruption problems that could arise as data grows.

- Concurrency Testing: Concurrency testing assesses the system's ability to handle multiple simultaneous users or transactions effectively. It helps identify issues related to data integrity, resource contention, and synchronization that might emerge in multi-user environments.
- Isolation Testing: Isolation testing involves testing individual components or subsystems in isolation to assess their performance characteristics independently. This methodology helps pinpoint performance bottlenecks at a granular level, aiding in targeted optimizations.
- Configuration Testing: Configuration testing evaluates the application's performance under different configurations, such as varying hardware setups, network conditions, or software versions. This methodology provides insights into the impact of different configurations on overall performance.
- Real-User Monitoring (RUM): RUM involves collecting and analyzing performance data from actual users' interactions with the application. This methodology offers real-world insights into user experience, enabling optimization based on genuine usage patterns.

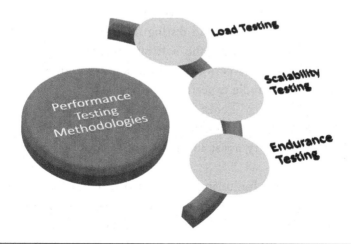

Performance testing methodologies.

4.2.1.2 Conclusion   The combination of various test levels and types ensures comprehensive testing coverage throughout the software development lifecycle. Each level and type serve a specific purpose, contributing to defect detection, validation of requirements, and overall software quality. By applying a mix of these testing approaches, organizations can deliver software that is robust, reliable, and aligned with user expectations.

4.2.2 Test Techniques and Tools

The test strategy also highlights specific test techniques and tools that will be employed. Manual testing is preferred for exploratory and usability.

While automated testing is suitable for regression and performance testing. Additionally, the strategy may identify specific test management tools, automation frameworks, and defect tracking systems to be used.

- Test Management Tools: Test management tools help manage and organize test cases, test plans, and test execution. They track testing progress, generate reports, and facilitate collaboration among team members.
- Automated Testing Tools: Automated testing tools automate the execution of test cases, reducing manual effort and increasing testing efficiency. They are particularly useful for regression testing and repetitive tasks.
- Load Testing Tools: Load testing tools simulate heavy user traffic to evaluate how the software performs under load. They help identify performance bottlenecks and ensure the software can handle expected user loads.
- Security Testing Tools: Security testing tools scan the software for vulnerabilities, security weaknesses, and potential threats. They assist in identifying security issues before deployment.
- Performance Monitoring Tools: Performance monitoring tools track and analyze the software's performance in real-time, providing insights into system behavior, resource usage, and response times.

- Code Analysis Tools: Code analysis tools review the source code for coding standards violations, potential defects, and adherence to best practices. They assist in ensuring code quality.
- Test Data Management Tools: Test data management tools help create, manage, and maintain test data sets for testing purposes. They ensure that test data is consistent, representative, and relevant.

CASE STUDY: EFFECTIVE TEST STRATEGY AT PRODIGY SYSTEMS INC.

In this case study, we explore how ABC Corporation formulated an effective test strategy and approach to ensure comprehensive testing coverage.

Example: Prodigy Systems Inc. adopted a risk-based testing approach for their projects. They identified critical areas and functionalities of the software that required extensive testing based on the potential impact of failures.

To support this strategy, Prodigy Systems Inc. combined both manual and automated testing techniques. Manual testing was preferred for exploratory and usability testing, while automated testing was utilized for regression and performance testing.

Prodigy Systems Inc. also invested in a test management tool to streamline test case management, test execution tracking, and test coverage monitoring.

Practical Exercise:

- Let's develop a test strategy and approach for a software project in your organization. Consider the following aspects:
- Identify the appropriate levels and types of testing based on project requirements and risk assessment.

- Determine the balance between manual and automated testing, considering time constraints, budget, and software complexity.
- Select the appropriate test techniques and tools to support testing efforts.
- Define a strategy for test data management, including data creation, data privacy, and data security considerations.
- Ensure that the test strategy aligns with the overall project objectives and constraints.

By formulating a clear test strategy and approach, you can ensure effective test coverage, optimized resource utilization, and the successful achievement of quality objectives.

4.3 Test Estimation and Scheduling

Test estimation and scheduling are critical for effective project planning. Estimation involves determining the effort and time required for testing activities, while scheduling ensures a well-organized timeline for test execution.

4.3.1 Test Effort Estimation

Estimating the test effort involves assessing the scope of testing, the complexity of the software, and the available resources. Several techniques, such as expert judgment and historical data analysis, can be employed for this purpose.

4.3.2 Test Schedule Creation

Creating a test schedule involves establishing a timeline for test execution, considering dependencies, milestones, and resource availability. This ensures that testing activities align with the overall project schedule.

CASE STUDY: EFFECTIVE TEST ESTIMATION AND SCHEDULING AT VISIONTECH ENTERPRISES

In this case study, we examine how DEF Corporation implemented effective test estimation and scheduling practices to ensure timely and efficient testing.

Example: VisionTech Enterprises adopted a bottom-up estimation approach for test effort estimation. They broke down testing activities into smaller tasks, estimated the effort required for each task, and aggregated the estimates to determine the overall test effort.

To create the test schedule, VisionTech Enterprises considered project milestones, resource availability, and dependencies. They allocated dedicated testing time for each level of testing, allowing sufficient time for defect fixing and retesting.

Practical Exercise:

- Let's estimate the test effort and create a test schedule for a software project in your organization. Follow these steps:
- Break down testing activities into smaller tasks, such as test case design, test execution, and defect tracking.
- Estimate the effort required for each task, considering factors like complexity, size, and available resources.
- Aggregate the task estimates to determine the overall test effort.
- Create a test schedule by allocating time for each testing activity, considering dependencies, milestones, and resource availability.
- Review and validate the test effort estimation and schedule with project stakeholders to ensure feasibility and alignment with project goals.

By accurately estimating test effort and creating a realistic test schedule, you can effectively plan and manage testing activities, ensuring timely delivery of high-quality software.

4.4 Test Metrics and Reporting

Test metrics and reporting are essential for monitoring and improving the quality of testing activities. They provide valuable insights into test coverage, defect density, and overall test effectiveness.

4.4.1 Test Metrics Selection

Selecting appropriate test metrics is crucial for evaluating the quality of the software and the effectiveness of testing efforts. Commonly used metrics include test case coverage, defect density, test execution status, and defect closure rate.

4.4.2 Test Reporting

Clear and concise test reporting is essential for effective communication of test results, progress, and quality status to project stakeholders. Test reports should highlight key metrics, identified defects, and any risks or issues.

CASE STUDY: EFFECTIVE TEST METRICS AND REPORTING AT AGILE INNOVATIONS CO.

In this case study, we explore how Agile Innovations Co. implemented effective test metrics and reporting practices to monitor and improve their testing efforts.

Example: Agile Innovations Co. defined and tracked various test metrics to measure the quality of their software. They regularly monitored test case coverage, defect density, and test execution status to assess the progress and effectiveness of their testing.

Test reports at Agile Innovations Co. provided a comprehensive overview of the test results, including key metrics, identified defects, and recommendations for improvement. The reports were shared with project stakeholders, facilitating informed decision-making, and ensuring transparency in the testing process.

Practical Exercise:

- Select appropriate test metrics and create a test report for a software project in your organization. Consider the following steps:
- Identify the key aspects of testing that need to be measured, such as test case coverage, defect density, or test execution progress.
- Determine the metrics that align with the project objectives and provide meaningful insights into the quality of the software.
- Establish a process for collecting and analyzing the required data to calculate the selected metrics.
- Design a test report format that effectively communicates the test results, including metrics, identified defects, and any recommendations.
- Share the test report with project stakeholders and seek their feedback for continuous improvement.

By implementing effective test metrics and reporting practices, you can monitor the progress, quality, and effectiveness of testing, enabling informed decision-making and facilitating continuous improvement.

In the next chapter, we will explore the process of defect management and how quality engineers can effectively identify, track, and resolve software defects throughout the testing lifecycle.

Note: This chapter focuses on test planning and management, providing detailed explanations, case studies, examples, and practical exercises. The inclusion of these elements aims to enhance understanding and enable the practical application of the concepts discussed. Subsequent chapters will delve deeper into specific aspects of software quality engineering to provide a comprehensive understanding of the field.

5

TEST AUTOMATION

5.1 Introduction to Test Automation

Test automation is a powerful technique that involves using tools and frameworks to automate the execution of test cases. Its goal is to enhance efficiency, reduce human errors, and increase test coverage. Test automation plays a vital role in the software testing process, bringing about a transformation in how testing activities are carried out and contributing to heightened efficiency, precision, and software quality. It involves employing automated testing tools and scripts to execute test cases, validate functionalities, and uncover defects. The significance of test automation spans across various phases of the development lifecycle. It accelerates the testing process, facilitates extensive test coverage, ensures consistency and reliability of results, and particularly excels in regression testing. By identifying defects early on, automation aids developers in resolving issues before they become more complex and costly. It frees up human testers from monotonous tasks, paving the way for more strategic and creative testing efforts. Test automation's impact is also felt in shorter development cycles, smoother integration into CI/CD pipelines, and the ability to handle complex scenarios and repetitive tasks with ease. It is a powerful investment that yields long-term benefits in terms of time saved, reduced manual effort, and elevated software quality. In this chapter, we will explore the concept of test automation and its numerous benefits.

5.1.1 Test Automation Overview

At the heart of test automation lies the creation and execution of automated test scripts, which simulate user interactions and validate

DOI: 10.1201/9781032702049-5

software functionality. This approach allows repetitive tests to be swiftly and consistently executed.

5.1.2 Benefits of Test Automation

Test automation offers a plethora of advantages, including improved test coverage, faster test execution, early detection of defects, and reduced human effort. Additionally, it facilitates regression testing, aids continuous integration and delivery, and elevates overall software quality. Let's walk through all of them in detail.

- Efficiency: Automated tests execute much faster than manual tests, enabling quicker feedback on code changes and facilitating faster development cycles. This efficiency results in reduced time-to-market and improved productivity.
- Increased Test Coverage: Automated tests can cover a wide range of scenarios, including edge cases and various configurations, ensuring comprehensive validation of software functionalities. This broader coverage helps detect defects that might be missed through manual testing.
- Consistency: Automated tests consistently perform the same steps and validations each time they are executed. This consistency eliminates human errors and ensures accurate results across multiple test runs.
- Regression Testing: Test automation excels in regression testing, allowing swift validation of existing functionalities when new code changes are introduced. It ensures that code updates do not inadvertently impact previously tested features.
- Resource Optimization: By automating repetitive and time-consuming tasks, human testers can focus on exploratory testing, critical thinking, and addressing complex scenarios that require human intuition and expertise.
- Early Defect Detection: Automated tests identify defects early in the development cycle, facilitating timely resolution and preventing issues from escalating to later stages, where they might be more challenging and costly to fix.
- Integration with CI/CD: Test automation seamlessly integrates with Continuous Integration and Continuous Delivery

(CI/CD) pipelines, providing quick feedback on code changes and enabling rapid, reliable software releases.

- Parallel Execution: Automated tests can run in parallel across multiple environments, configurations, or devices, enhancing testing efficiency and shortening testing cycles.
- Scalability: Test automation is scalable, allowing testing efforts to be easily expanded to accommodate larger projects, more frequent releases, and increased testing demands.
- Documentation and Reporting: Automated tests generate detailed logs and reports, providing clear documentation of test results, defects, and test coverage. These reports aid in communication and decision-making.
- Cost Efficiency: While there is an initial investment in setting up automation frameworks and scripts, the long-term savings in terms of reduced manual effort, faster testing cycles, and enhanced software quality outweigh the costs.
- Continuous Improvement: Test automation encourages the development of reusable test scripts and frameworks, fostering a culture of continuous improvement in testing practices and processes.

5.1.3 Challenges in Test Automation: Navigating Complexity and Optimization

While test automation offers numerous benefits, it also presents certain challenges that testing teams must navigate to ensure successful implementation. Overcoming these challenges is crucial for maximizing the effectiveness of automated testing efforts. Here are some common challenges in test automation.

- Initial Investment: Implementing test automation requires an upfront investment of time, effort, and resources to set up automation frameworks, scripts, and tools.
- Test Selection: Determining which test cases to automate and which to leave for manual testing can be challenging. Not all tests are suitable candidates for automation, and making the right choices is essential.

- Script Maintenance: Automated test scripts require ongoing maintenance to adapt to changes in the application, such as UI modifications or feature updates. Keeping scripts up to date can be time-consuming.
- Tool Selection: Choosing the right testing tools that align with project requirements, technical stack, and testing goals can be overwhelming. Tool evaluation and selection require careful consideration.
- Test Data Management: Managing test data for automated tests, including data setup and cleanup, can be complex. Ensuring accurate and relevant test data is critical for test execution.
- Dynamic Environments: Automated tests may face challenges in dynamic environments where elements' identifiers change frequently, leading to test script failures.
- Flakiness: Automated tests can be sensitive to environmental variations, resulting in intermittent failures (flakiness). Dealing with flaky tests requires investigation and troubleshooting.
- Complex Scenarios: Automated tests may struggle with complex scenarios that involve intricate business logic, making test script design and maintenance more challenging.
- Skills and Training: Test automation requires specialized skills in scripting languages, automation tools, and frameworks. Teams may need training to effectively utilize these resources.
- Parallel Execution: Coordinating and managing tests running in parallel across different configurations and environments can be complex and require synchronization mechanisms.
- Non-Functional Testing: While automated testing excels in functional testing, addressing non-functional aspects like performance, security, and usability can be more intricate.
- Limited Usability Testing: Automation might not capture all usability aspects, as certain user experience elements are better evaluated through manual testing.
- Initial Learning Curve: Teams transitioning from manual to automated testing may initially experience a learning curve as they familiarize themselves with automation concepts and practices.

- Overemphasis on Coverage: Focusing solely on achieving high test coverage through automation can lead to neglecting critical test scenarios and potential defects.
- Return on Investment (ROI) Calculation: Measuring the ROI of test automation, particularly in terms of time saved and defects detected, can be complex but is essential for justifying automation efforts.

5.1.4 When to Consider Test Automation

Deciding when to implement test automation is a strategic choice based on stable requirements, repetitive testing needs, regression testing requirements, long testing cycles, consistent test cases, large data sets, parallel testing needs, integration with CI/CD pipelines, scalability demands, complexity of scenarios, resource optimization goals, anticipated ROI, project longevity, and availability of skilled resources. Introducing automation at these points optimizes testing efficiency, accelerates feedback cycles, enhances coverage, and ensures high software quality, aligning automation efforts with project goals and characteristics. "Often, the most important thing you can do during the design period is to identify testing support code that you want in the program (or with it). You might not get this support, but if you ask early, and explain the value of the individual tools clearly, you stand a good chance of getting some of them" [5].

CASE STUDY: SUCCESSFUL TEST AUTOMATION IMPLEMENTATION AT FIRSTCHOICE TECHNOLOGIES

Let's explore how FirstChoice Technologies effectively implemented test automation to enhance their testing efficiency and effectiveness.

Example: FirstChoice Technologies identified repetitive test cases in their regression suite that were ideal candidates for automation. They developed automated test scripts using popular test automation tools and seamlessly integrated them into their test execution process. The result was remarkable time savings and an enhancement in the accuracy and reliability of their tests.

Practical Exercise:

- In your organization, identify test cases suitable for automation using the following steps:
- Review your existing test suite and identify frequently executed or repetitive test cases.
- Assess the feasibility of automating these test cases, considering factors such as complexity, stability, and expected ROI.
- Select a suitable test automation tool or framework based on your project requirements and technical environment.
- Develop automated test scripts for the identified test cases and seamlessly integrate them into your test execution process.
- Execute the automated test scripts and compare the results with manual test execution to validate the effectiveness of test automation.

By implementing test automation, you can streamline your testing process, improve efficiency, and achieve higher test coverage.

5.2 Frameworks and Tools for Test Automation

Test automation frameworks and tools provide a structured approach and the necessary resources for developing and executing automated test scripts. Let's delve into some popular frameworks and tools used in test automation.

5.2.1 Test Automation Frameworks

Test automation frameworks offer a structured and systematic approach to test automation. They provide guidelines, templates, and libraries that simplify test script development, execution, and maintenance. Commonly used frameworks include keyword-driven frameworks, data-driven frameworks, and behavior-driven frameworks. Here's an overview of common test automation frameworks.

Modular Framework: The modular framework divides the automation project into smaller, independent modules or functions. Each module focuses on testing specific functionalities. This approach enhances reusability, as modules can be easily reused across different test scenarios.

- Data-Driven Framework: In the data-driven framework, test data is stored externally, allowing tests to be executed with different input data sets. This approach enhances test coverage by enabling the same test case to be executed with various data combinations.

- Keyword-Driven Framework: Keyword-driven frameworks separate test design and test execution. Test cases are written using keywords that represent actions, and these keywords are mapped to corresponding code scripts. This approach promotes collaboration between technical and non-technical testers.

- Hybrid Framework: The hybrid framework combines elements of various frameworks, tailoring the approach to the project's requirements. It leverages the strengths of different frameworks to accommodate diverse testing needs.

- Page Object Model (POM): The POM framework models each web page as a class, encapsulating its elements and interactions. This approach promotes reusability, readability, and maintenance of test scripts, particularly for web applications.

- Behavior-Driven Development (BDD): BDD frameworks focus on collaboration among developers, testers, and domain experts. They use a natural language syntax to define test scenarios, making tests more readable and understandable.

- TestNG and JUnit Frameworks: These frameworks provide unit testing capabilities for Java applications. They offer features like parallel execution, test grouping, and parameterization.

- Robot Framework: Robot Framework is an open-source, keyword-driven testing framework. It supports both web and desktop applications and provides extensive libraries and integrations.

- Appium and Espresso (Mobile Testing Frameworks): Appium (for cross-platform) and Espresso (for Android) are popular frameworks for mobile app testing. They allow automated testing of mobile applications on various devices and platforms.

- Protractor (AngularJS Testing Framework): The contractor is designed specifically for testing AngularJS applications. It integrates with Jasmine and supports end-to-end testing.
- Cucumber (BDD Framework): Cucumber is a BDD framework that supports multiple programming languages. It promotes collaboration through feature files written in a human-readable format.
- Selenium WebDriver: Selenium WebDriver is a widely used automation tool for web applications. It provides APIs to interact with web elements and simulate user actions.
- Test Complete: Test Complete is a commercial tool that supports automated testing for web, desktop, mobile, and APIs. It offers a variety of built-in features and integrations.

5.2.2 Conclusion

Test automation frameworks play a crucial role in structuring and optimizing automation efforts. The choice of framework depends on project requirements, application characteristics, and team expertise. Implementing a suitable framework enhances testing efficiency, reusability, and collaboration, leading to more effective automation outcomes.

5.2.3 Test Automation Tools

Test automation tools empower the creation and execution of automated test scripts. They offer features for recording, playback, and debugging test scripts, as well as reporting and integration capabilities. Some popular test automation tools include Selenium, Appium, JUnit, TestNG, and Cucumber.

5.2.4 Components of a Test Automation Framework

A well-structured test automation framework comprises several essential components that work together to streamline test script development, execution, and management. These components form the building blocks of a cohesive and efficient automation solution. Here are the key components that make up a comprehensive test automation framework.

- Test Scripts: Test scripts are the heart of the framework, containing the actual code that simulates user interactions and validates application behavior. These scripts are written using programming languages and automation libraries.
- Test Data Management: This component handles the storage, retrieval, and management of test data used in test scripts. It includes mechanisms to generate, manipulate, and store test data for different scenarios.
- Object Repository: The object repository stores information about application elements (UI controls, widgets, APIs) in a centralized manner. This repository simplifies script maintenance by separating element identification from test scripts.
- Test Execution Engine: The test execution engine executes the test scripts, interacts with application elements through the object repository, and reports test results. It manages the flow of test execution.
- Reporting and Logging: This component generates detailed test execution reports and logs, providing insights into test outcomes, defects, and coverage. Comprehensive reporting aids in analysis and decision-making.
- Test Framework Libraries: Test framework libraries consist of reusable functions, methods, and utilities that abstract common testing tasks. These libraries simplify test script creation and promote consistency.
- Configuration Management: Configuration management handles settings and configurations that influence test execution, such as browser selection, environment parameters, and database connections.
- Test Case Management: Test case management involves organizing and categorizing test cases, grouping them based on features or functionalities. This component facilitates test organization and execution planning.

- Test Environment Management: Test environment management involves configuring and maintaining testing environments that replicate production conditions. It ensures accurate testing results and minimizes environment-related issues.
- Continuous Integration (CI) Integration: This component integrates the framework with CI/CD tools, enabling automated test execution within the CI pipeline. It ensures that tests are executed consistently with code changes.
- Error Handling and Recovery: Error handling mechanisms manage exceptions and errors that occur during test execution. They provide graceful recovery and generate informative error messages.
- Version Control Integration: Version control integration with tools like Git allows teams to manage and track changes to framework code and test scripts. It facilitates collaboration and code rollbacks.
- Test Execution Scheduler: The test execution scheduler automates the scheduling and execution of tests at specific times or intervals. It's useful for running tests during non-peak hours.
- Cross-Browser and Cross-Platform Support: This component ensures that tests can be executed across various browsers, operating systems, and devices, maintaining consistent functionality.
- Collaboration and Reporting Integration: Integration with collaboration and reporting tools enables seamless communication among team members, stakeholders, and management regarding test progress and outcomes.

5.2.5 Conclusion

Each of these components contributes to the effectiveness, efficiency, and scalability of a test automation framework. By designing and integrating these components cohesively, testing teams can establish a powerful automation solution that optimizes testing efforts, enhances software quality, and accelerates delivery timelines.

CASE STUDY: EFFECTIVE USE OF THE TEST AUTOMATION FRAMEWORK AT DATA TECH SYSTEMS

Let's explore how Data Tech Systems successfully implemented a test automation framework to streamline their test automation efforts.

Example: Data Tech Systems adopted a data-driven framework for their test automation. By separating test data from test scripts, they achieved easy maintenance and scalability.

The framework provided reusable components and libraries, simplifying test script development, and enhancing code reusability.

Practical Exercise:

- Select a test automation framework and tool for a software project in your organization using the following steps:
- Evaluate the project requirements, test objectives, and technical environment to identify the most suitable framework and tool.
- Research and compare different frameworks and tools based on factors such as features, community support, and compatibility with your technology stack.
- Implement the chosen framework and tool in your testing environment.
- Develop a sample automated test script using the framework and tool, considering best practices and guidelines.
- Execute the test script and assess the effectiveness and efficiency of the chosen framework and tool.

By leveraging test automation frameworks and tools, you can streamline test script development, execution, and maintenance, resulting in improved test efficiency and productivity.

5.3 Selecting Test Cases for Automation

Selecting the right test cases for automation is crucial for a successful test automation effort. Let's explore some guidelines for identifying test cases suitable for automation.

5.3.1 Test Case Selection Criteria

Test cases suitable for automation should meet specific criteria, such as repeatability, stability, and high regression risk. Test cases with clear steps, predictable results, and a high likelihood of encountering defects are good candidates for automation.

5.3.2 Prioritization of Test Cases

To start a test automation effort, prioritize test cases based on factors like business criticality, complexity, and frequency of execution. Begin with a subset of test cases that provide maximum coverage and value.

CASE STUDY: EFFECTIVE TEST CASE SELECTION FOR AUTOMATION AT VISIONARY ENTERPRISES LTD.

Let's explore how Visionary Enterprises Ltd. implemented a systematic approach to test case selection for automation.

Example: Visionary Enterprises Ltd. prioritized test cases for automation based on the risk associated with the software functionalities and the frequency of execution. They started by automating high-priority test cases with high regression risk, ensuring maximum coverage of critical functionalities.

Practical Exercise:

- Select test cases for automation in your organization using the following steps:

- Review your test suite and identify test cases that meet the criteria for automation, such as repeatability, stability, and high regression risk.
- Prioritize the identified test cases based on factors like business criticality, complexity, and frequency of execution.
- Develop automated test scripts for the selected test cases using the chosen test automation tool and framework.
- Execute the automated test scripts and compare the results with manual test execution to validate the effectiveness of automation.

By selecting the right test cases for automation, you can maximize the benefits of test automation and achieve efficient and effective test execution.

5.4 Test Automation Best Practices

Adhering to best practices is essential for successful test automation. Let's explore a set of best practices that should be followed during test automation efforts.

5.4.1 Planning and Strategy

Establish a clear test automation strategy, including goals, objectives, and expected outcomes. Plan for test script development, maintenance, and execution, considering factors like resource allocation, timelines, and scalability.

5.4.2 Test Script Design

Follow good design principles to create modular, maintainable, and reusable test scripts. Use proper naming conventions, abstraction, and parameterization to enhance script readability and maintainability.

5.4.3 Test Data Management

Separate test data from test scripts and employ appropriate data management techniques. Use data-driven approaches to handle multiple test scenarios efficiently.

5.4.4 Test Execution and Reporting

Execute automated tests in a controlled environment, ensuring the availability of necessary test data and configurations. Capture and analyze test execution results to identify failures, trends, and areas for improvement.

CASE STUDY: SUCCESSFUL IMPLEMENTATION OF TEST AUTOMATION BEST PRACTICES AT GLOBAL TECH INDUSTRIES

Let's explore how Global Tech Industries implemented test automation best practices to achieve efficient and effective test automation.

Example: Global Tech Industries followed a well-defined test automation strategy, considering the scalability of their automation efforts. They designed test scripts following modular and reusable design principles, enabling easy maintenance and reusability. Global Tech Industries also adopted a data-driven approach to manage test data effectively.

Practical Exercise:

- Implement test automation best practices in your organization using the following steps:
- Develop a test automation strategy that aligns with your project objectives and goals.
- Design test scripts following modular and reusable design principles, incorporating proper naming conventions, abstraction, and parameterization.
- Implement appropriate test data management techniques, separating test data from test scripts, and utilizing data-driven approaches.

- Execute automated tests in a controlled environment, capturing and analyzing test execution results.
- Review and refine your test automation process based on the insights gained from test execution and reporting.

By following test automation best practices, you can ensure the effectiveness, scalability, and maintainability of your test automation efforts.

In the next chapter, we will explore the process of test execution and defect management, highlighting techniques and practices for efficient defect identification, tracking, and resolution.

Note: This chapter focuses on test automation, providing detailed explanations, case studies, examples, and practical exercises. The inclusion of these elements aims to enhance understanding and enable practical application of the concepts discussed. Subsequent chapters will delve deeper into specific aspects of software quality engineering to provide a comprehensive understanding of the field.

6

PERFORMANCE TESTING

6.1 The Significance of Performance Testing

Performance testing is an essential aspect of software quality engineering that concentrates on evaluating a software system's performance, scalability, and reliability under various load conditions. This chapter emphasizes the importance of performance testing and its impact on ensuring software quality.

6.1.1 Overview of Performance Testing

Performance testing entails assessing the responsiveness, stability, and resource usage of a software system. Its primary goal is to identify performance bottlenecks, uncover system limitations, and ensure that the application meets performance expectations.

6.1.2 Benefits of Performance Testing

The benefits of performance testing are numerous.

Notably, it allows for the early detection of performance issues, the optimization of system resources, an improved user experience, and enhanced customer satisfaction. By preventing performance-related failures, ensuring system stability, and facilitating effective capacity planning, performance testing plays a pivotal role in creating robust software.

CASE STUDY: SUCCESSFUL PERFORMANCE TESTING AT INNOVATIVE SOLUTION CO.

This case study delves into how Innovative Solutions Co. successfully utilized performance testing to achieve optimal performance and scalability for their e-commerce platform.

DOI: 10.1201/9781032702049-6

Example: Prior to a major sales event, **Innovative Solutions Co.** conducted performance testing on their e-commerce platform by simulating high user loads. Through this process, they identified performance bottlenecks and optimized their system to handle increased traffic. Consequently, they handled the surge in users without experiencing any performance degradation.

Practical Exercise:

Embark on a performance test for a software system within your organization by following these steps:

- Identify performance objectives and success criteria for the test, such as response time, throughput, and resource utilization.
- Select appropriate performance testing techniques and tools based on the system architecture and test requirements.
- Define realistic workload scenarios that simulate expected user behavior and load conditions.
- Execute the performance test, monitor system performance, and collect relevant performance metrics.
- Analyze the test results, identify performance bottlenecks, and prioritize optimization opportunities.
- Optimize the system based on the identified issues and rerun the performance test to validate improvements.

Through conducting performance testing, you can ensure that your software system performs optimally under various load conditions, providing a high-quality user experience.

6.2 Performance Testing Techniques and Tools

This section explores various techniques and tools utilized in performance testing to effectively evaluate a software system's performance.

6.2.1 Performance Testing Techniques

Performance testing techniques include load testing, stress testing, and scalability testing. Load testing assesses system performance under expected load conditions; stress testing pushes the system beyond its limits to identify breaking points; and scalability testing measures the system's ability to handle increasing workloads.

6.2.2 Performance Testing Tools

Performance testing tools play a crucial role in creating realistic workload scenarios, generating virtual users, measuring system response times, and analyzing performance metrics. Some popular performance testing tools are Apache JMeter, LoadRunner, and Gatling. Performance testing tools are indispensable in evaluating the responsiveness, scalability, and stability of software applications under different workloads and conditions. These tools simulate user interactions, stress the system, and provide insights into performance bottlenecks. Here are some prominent performance testing tools:

- Apache JMeter: Apache JMeter is an open-source tool for load testing, stress testing, and performance testing. It supports various protocols, including HTTP, HTTPS, FTP, and more. JMeter allows users to simulate a high number of users and monitor system behavior.
- LoadRunner: LoadRunner by Micro Focus is a widely used performance testing tool. It offers a comprehensive suite of testing capabilities, including load testing, stress testing, and performance monitoring. It supports various application protocols and provides in-depth analysis of test results.
- Gatling: Gatling is an open-source load testing tool known for its simplicity and efficiency. It uses a lightweight Domain-Specific Language for test script creation and supports HTTP, WebSocket, and other protocols.
- Apache Benchmark (ab): Apache Benchmark, commonly known as "ab," is a command-line tool provided by the Apache HTTP server project. It's used for simple load testing and measures the performance of web servers and applications.

- BlazeMeter: BlazeMeter offers cloud-based performance testing solutions. It supports a variety of testing types, including load testing, stress testing, and scalability testing. BlazeMeter enables easy test script creation and offers real-time analytics.
- Locust: Locust is an open-source load testing tool that focuses on simplicity and extensibility. It uses a Python-based scripting approach and allows users to define user behavior through code.
- Apache Benchmark (ab): Apache Benchmark, commonly known as "ab," is a command-line tool provided by the Apache HTTP server project. It's used for simple load testing and measures the performance of web servers and applications.
- Apache Benchmark (ab): Apache Benchmark, commonly known as "ab," is a command-line tool provided by the Apache HTTP server project. It's used for simple load testing and measures the performance of web servers and applications.
- NeoLoad: NeoLoad offers load testing, stress testing, and performance testing capabilities. It supports a wide range of protocols, including HTTP, WebSockets, and mobile. NeoLoad provides real-time monitoring and analysis of test results.
- Silk Performer: Silk Performer by Micro Focus is a perform-ance testing tool that supports a variety of application environments, including web, mobile, and cloud. It offers in-depth analysis and diagnostics for performance issues.
- Rational Performance Tester: Rational Performance Tester by IBM is a tool for load testing, stress testing, and scalability testing. It integrates with other IBM Rational tools and provides script creation, execution, and analysis features.
- Web LOAD: Web LOAD by RadView is a load testing tool that supports a range of applications, protocols, and technolo-gies. It provides real-time monitoring and analysis of test results and supports both cloud and on-premises deployments.

Conclusion: Performance testing tools are essential for assessing application performance and identifying potential issues that might arise under different conditions. These tools enable organizations to optimize software performance, ensure a seamless user experience, and deliver high-quality applications to users.

CASE STUDY: EFFECTIVE USE OF PERFORMANCE TESTING TOOLS AT INNOVATIVE SOLUTIONS CO.

This case study explores how Innovative Solutions Co. effectively employed performance testing tools to evaluate and optimize their web application's performance.

Example: Innovative Solutions Co. leveraged Apache JMeter to simulate realistic user loads and measure response times for their web application. Through analysis of performance metrics, they identified bottlenecks and optimized their application, resulting in improved response times and scalability.

Practical Exercise:

Select a performance testing technique and tool for a software system in your organization by following these steps:

1. Determine the appropriate performance testing technique based on your system's requirements and objectives.
2. Research and compare different performance testing tools, considering factors such as features, scalability, ease of use, and compatibility with your technology stack.
3. Set up and configure the chosen performance testing tool to create realistic workload scenarios.
4. Execute the performance test, monitor system performance, and collect relevant performance metrics.
5. Analyze the test results, identify performance issues, and explore ways to optimize the system.

By utilizing performance testing techniques and tools, you can evaluate and enhance the performance of your software system, ensuring an optimal user experience and system scalability.

6.3 Performance Test Planning and Execution

This section focuses on the process of effectively planning and executing performance tests, considering factors such as test environment setup, workload creation, and result analysis.

6.3.1 Performance Test Planning

Performance test planning involves defining test objectives, identifying performance metrics, establishing test criteria, and creating a test plan. Additionally, it includes setting up the test environment, including hardware, software, and network configurations, to closely resemble the production environment.

6.3.2 Performance Test Execution

Performance test execution involves running the planned test scenarios, monitoring system performance, collecting performance metrics, and analyzing the results. This phase requires careful configuration of the performance testing tool and accurate simulation of realistic workload scenarios.

CASE STUDY: SUCCESSFUL PERFORMANCE TEST PLANNING AND EXECUTION AT VERTEX SERVICES LTD

This case study examines how Vertex Services Ltd meticulously planned and executed performance tests to ensure the scalability and reliability of their cloud-based application.

Example: Vertex Services Ltd set clear objectives, identified critical performance metrics, and created realistic workload scenarios during their performance tests. They executed the tests in a controlled environment, closely monitored system performance, and collected relevant performance metrics. Analyzing the test results helped them identify performance bottlenecks and optimize their application.

Practical Exercise:
Plan and execute a performance test for a software system in your organization by following these steps:

1. Define the objectives, success criteria, and performance metrics for the performance test.

2. Set up the test environment, ensuring it closely resembles the production environment in terms of hardware, software, and network configurations.
3. Create realistic workload scenarios based on expected user behavior and load conditions.
4. Configure the performance testing tool to simulate the workload scenarios and execute the performance test.
5. Monitor system performance during the test execution and collect relevant performance metrics.
6. Analyze the test results, identify performance bottlenecks, and explore optimization opportunities.

By effectively planning and executing performance tests, you can proactively identify and address performance issues, ensuring a high-performing and scalable software system.

6.4 Performance Test Analysis and Optimization

This section focuses on analyzing performance test results, identifying performance bottlenecks, and optimizing system performance based on the findings.

6.4.1 Performance Test Analysis

Performance test analysis entails examining performance metrics, identifying bottlenecks, and understanding the root causes of performance issues. It requires comparing actual performance against the defined performance objectives and success criteria.

6.4.2 Performance Optimization

Performance optimization aims to enhance system performance by addressing identified bottlenecks. This may involve code optimization, database tuning, infrastructure scaling, or caching mechanisms. The effectiveness of optimization efforts should be validated through subsequent performance tests.

CASE STUDY: EFFECTIVE PERFORMANCE TEST ANALYSIS AND OPTIMIZATION AT APEX INNOVATIONS

This case study explores how **Apex Innovations** analyzed performance test results, identified bottlenecks, and optimized the performance of their enterprise application.

Example: Apex Innovations utilized performance monitoring tools to analyze test results and identify database-related performance bottlenecks. They optimized database queries, implemented caching mechanisms, and fine-tuned database configurations. Subsequent performance tests showed significant improvements in system response times and scalability.

Practical Exercise:

Analyze performance test results for a software system in your organization and identify performance bottlenecks by following these steps:

- Review the performance test results and compare them against the defined performance objectives and success criteria.
- Identify performance bottlenecks by analyzing performance metrics such as response times, throughput, and resource utilization.
- Investigate the root causes of the identified performance issues, considering factors like code efficiency, database queries, and network latency or hardware limitations.
- Develop a performance optimization plan based on the identified bottlenecks, considering techniques such as code optimization, infrastructure scaling, or caching mechanisms.
- Implement the identified optimizations and rerun the performance tests to validate the improvements.

Through effective performance test analysis and optimization, you can ensure that your software system meets performance requirements, delivers a seamless user experience, and supports scalability. "Collaboration among cross-functional teams and the iterative refinement of test scenarios stand as cornerstones in overcoming the challenges of performance testing. By fostering an environment of shared knowledge, open communication, and collective problem-solving, organizations can navigate complex scenarios and ensure that their performance-testing efforts yield accurate and actionable insights. This collaborative approach not only enhances application performance but also fosters a culture of continuous improvement throughout the software development lifecycle" [6].

In the next chapter, we will explore the field of security testing, focusing on techniques and practices to assess the security and robustness of software systems.

7

SECURITY TESTING

7.1 Understanding Software Security

Software security plays a critical role in software quality engineering, focusing on the identification and mitigation of potential security vulnerabilities to safeguard sensitive data. This chapter provides an overview of software security and its significance in today's digital landscape.

7.1.1 Introduction to Software Security

Software security is the practice of safeguarding software systems and data from unauthorized access, breaches, and malicious attacks. It involves the implementation of security measures and practices to ensure the confidentiality, integrity, and availability of information.

7.1.2 Importance of Software Security

The importance of software security cannot be overstated, as it directly impacts user trust, protects sensitive information, ensures regulatory compliance, and prevents financial and reputational damage. In our interconnected world, where cyber threats abound, software security is an absolute necessity for any organization.

7.1.3 Defining Security Testing and its Significance in Modern Software

Security testing is a crucial aspect of software development that focuses on assessing the security vulnerabilities and weaknesses of an application, system, or network. It involves a systematic evaluation of software components to identify potential

DOI: 10.1201/9781032702049-7

vulnerabilities, threats, and risks that could compromise the confidentiality, integrity, and availability of sensitive information and functionalities. Security testing aims to uncover vulnerabilities that attackers might exploit to gain unauthorized access, steal data, disrupt services, or compromise the overall security posture of the software.

In modern software development, security testing holds immense significance due to several compelling reasons.

- Growing Cybersecurity Threats: With the increasing complexity of software systems and the rise of sophisticated cyber threats, security vulnerabilities have become more prevalent. Security testing helps identify and mitigate potential entry points for attackers.
- Protecting User Data: Applications often handle sensitive user data, such as personal information, financial details, and login credentials. Security breaches can lead to data leaks and privacy violations. Effective security testing ensures the protection of user information.
- Legal and Regulatory Compliance: Many industries are subject to stringent data protection regulations, such as GDPR, HIPAA, and PCI DSS. Non-compliance can result in severe penalties. Security testing helps ensure adherence to these regulations.
- Reputation and Trust: Security breaches can seriously damage a company's reputation and erode customer trust. Regular security testing helps build and maintain customer confidence in the software's security measures.
- Financial Implications: Addressing security vulnerabilities after deployment can be costly and time-consuming. It's more cost-effective to identify and rectify security issues during the development phase through testing.
- Integrated Development Practices: Modern development practices, such as DevOps and Continuous Integration/Continuous Deployment (CI/CD), emphasize rapid software releases. Security testing integrated into these practices ensures that security remains a priority throughout the development lifecycle.

- Threat Landscape Evolution: Cyber threats and attack vectors evolve rapidly. Regular security testing helps organizations stay proactive by identifying new vulnerabilities and adapting security measures accordingly.
- Third-Party Components: Many applications rely on third-party libraries and components. Security testing helps identify vulnerabilities in these components, reducing the risk of incorporating insecure code.
- Internet of Things (IoT) Security: As IoT devices become more prevalent, the potential attack surface increases. Security testing ensures that IoT devices and their communication channels are adequately protected.
- Complex Architectures: Modern software architectures, like microservices and cloud computing, introduce new challenges in terms of security. Security testing helps identify vulnerabilities that might arise in these complex environments.

7.1.4 Conclusion

In conclusion, security testing is a critical practice in modern software development to safeguard applications and systems against evolving cyber threats. It ensures the protection of sensitive data, compliance with regulations, and the establishment of a strong security posture. By integrating security testing into the development process, organizations can proactively address vulnerabilities, reduce risks, and enhance the overall security and reliability of their software products.

7.1.5 Emphasizing the Importance of Safeguarding Sensitive Information and Data

Protecting sensitive information and data is paramount in today's interconnected digital landscape. As technology advances and our lives become more intertwined with digital platforms, the significance of safeguarding sensitive data cannot be overstated. Here's why it's crucial.

- Data Privacy: Sensitive information includes personal, financial, and health-related data. Ensuring its privacy is essential to prevent unauthorized access, identity theft, and potential misuse.

- User Trust: Organizations that prioritize data protection build trust with their users. When individuals trust that their information is secure, they are more likely to engage with and use digital services.
- Legal and Regulatory Compliance: Data protection regulations like GDPR, HIPAA, and CCPA mandate strict measures to safeguard sensitive data. Failure to comply can result in hefty fines and legal consequences.
- Business Reputation: Data breaches can lead to irreparable damage to an organization's reputation. News of a breach spreads quickly and can result in loss of customers and stakeholders.
- Intellectual Property: Companies often possess proprietary information critical to their success. Protecting this intellectual property ensures competitors cannot gain an unfair advantage.
- Financial Security: Sensitive financial data, such as credit card details and banking information, must be safeguarded to prevent financial losses and fraudulent activities.
- Healthcare and Medical Data: Medical records are highly sensitive, and breaches can compromise patient privacy and safety. Proper protection is vital for healthcare providers and patients alike.
- Preventing Cybercrime: Cybercriminals constantly seek to exploit vulnerabilities for financial gain or other malicious purposes. Robust security measures deter such activities.
- Trust in Digital Services: In an increasingly digital world, individuals rely on online services for banking, shopping, communication, and more. Ensuring data security fosters trust in these services.
- Employee Data: Protecting employee data, including payroll and personal information, is critical for maintaining a healthy work environment and complying with labor laws.
- National Security: In certain cases, sensitive data pertains to national security. Safeguarding this information is vital for maintaining the security of nations.

- Mitigating Insider Threats: Internal personnel can also pose risks. Implementing proper access controls and monitoring helps prevent unauthorized data access.
- Long-Term Viability: Companies that prioritize data security establish themselves as responsible and forward-thinking entities, contributing to their long-term success.

In essence, safeguarding sensitive information is not just a legal obligation; it's an ethical responsibility that affects individuals, organizations, and society as a whole. Prioritizing data security promotes trust, compliance, and reputation and ultimately contributes to the well-being of individuals and the integrity of digital ecosystems.

CASE STUDY: SUCCESSFUL IMPLEMENTATION OF SOFTWARE SECURITY MEASURES AT SECURETECH CORPORATION

In this case study, we examine how **SecureTech Corporation** effectively implemented robust software security measures to protect their customer data and ensure the integrity of their software systems.

Example: SecureTech Corporation employed encryption algorithms to secure sensitive data transmission, conducted regular security assessments and audits, and enforced strict access control policies. As a result, they successfully protected their systems from unauthorized access and maintained their customers' trust.

7.2 Types of Security Testing

Security testing encompasses various techniques aimed at identifying vulnerabilities, weaknesses, and potential threats within software applications, systems, and networks. Each type of security testing serves a specific purpose in ensuring the confidentiality, integrity, and availability of sensitive data and functionalities. Here are some key types of security testing.

- Vulnerability Assessment: Vulnerability assessment involves systematically scanning software and networks to identify known vulnerabilities and weaknesses. Automated tools and manual analysis are used to detect potential entry points for attackers. "Vulnerability scanning employs automated tools to detect known security vulnerabilities within an application's codebase, infrastructure, or dependencies. These tools systematically analyze software components and configurations, highlighting weaknesses that could be exploited. Vulnerability scanning provides a rapid assessment of potential risks and helps prioritize necessary patches or mitigations" [7].
- Penetration Testing (Pen Testing): Penetration testing simulates real-world attacks to assess the system's security measures. Skilled testers attempt to exploit vulnerabilities, gaining unauthorized access to identify weak points that need strengthening.
- Security Scanning: Security scanning tools examine applications and networks for security flaws. This includes scanning for open ports, misconfigured settings, and potential vulnerabilities that could be exploited.
- Security Auditing: Security auditing involves a comprehensive review of the system's security controls, policies, and procedures. It ensures that security measures are aligned with best practices and industry standards.
- Code Review: Code review, also known as static analysis, examines the source code for vulnerabilities, insecure coding practices, and potential threats. It helps identify security issues at the code level.
- Security Architecture Review: This review assesses the design and architecture of the application or system from a security perspective. It ensures that security measures are embedded within the design itself.

Types of security testing.

- Fuzz Testing (Fuzzing): Fuzz testing involves sending unexpected, invalid, or random data to the application to uncover vulnerabilities caused by input errors or unexpected data formats.
- SQL Injection Testing: SQL injection testing identifies vulnerabilities that allow attackers to manipulate a system's database by injecting malicious SQL queries through input fields.
- Cross-Site Scripting (XSS) Testing: XSS testing detects vulnerabilities that allow attackers to inject malicious scripts

into web applications. These scripts can be executed in users' browsers, compromising their data.

- Cross-Site Request Forgery (CSRF) Testing: CSRF testing identifies vulnerabilities that allow attackers to execute unauthorized actions on behalf of authenticated users, potentially leading to data manipulation or theft.
- Authentication and Authorization Testing: This testing ensures that authentication and authorization mechanisms are robust, preventing unauthorized access to sensitive data and functionalities.
- Session Management Testing: Session management testing assesses how the application handles user sessions, ensuring that session data is secure and that sessions are properly terminated.
- Encryption Testing: Encryption testing examines the implementation of encryption mechanisms to ensure that sensitive data is securely transmitted and stored.
- Mobile Application Security Testing: This testing focuses on identifying vulnerabilities specific to mobile applications, such as insecure storage of data, lack of secure communication, and potential data leakage.
- IoT Security Testing: IoT security testing evaluates the security of IoT devices and their communication channels to prevent potential vulnerabilities.

In conclusion, various types of security testing are essential for identifying vulnerabilities and ensuring the robustness of software applications, systems, and networks. By systematically addressing potential security risks, organizations can enhance their defenses and provide a secure environment for their users and data.

7.3 Security Testing Process

The security testing process is a systematic approach to assessing software applications, systems, and networks for vulnerabilities, weaknesses, and potential threats that could compromise their integrity and confidentiality. This process aims to identify security risks and provide actionable insights to strengthen an application's defenses. Here's an overview of the security testing process.

- Requirement Analysis: Understand the application's security requirements, business context, and potential threats. Define the scope of testing, including functionalities, user roles, and data flows.
- Threat Modeling: Identify potential threats and vulnerabilities by analyzing the application's architecture and design. Consider potential attack vectors, data flows, and access points that attackers might exploit.
- Test Planning: Create a comprehensive security test plan that outlines testing objectives, methodologies, tools, resources, and timelines. Define the testing approach for each type of security testing to be conducted.
- Test Environment Setup: Set up the testing environment, which should mirror the production environment as closely as possible. This includes configuring servers, databases, networks, and other components.
- Security Test Design: Design security test cases based on the identified threats and vulnerabilities. Develop tests for different attack vectors, including input validation, authentication, authorization, and more.
- Test Execution: Execute the security test cases according to the test plan. Use automated tools and manual techniques to simulate attacks, attempt unauthorized access, and evaluate the application's response.
- Vulnerability Analysis: Analyze the test results to identify vulnerabilities, security weaknesses, and potential entry points for attackers. Prioritize vulnerabilities based on severity and potential impact.
- Remediation: Provide recommendations for addressing the identified vulnerabilities. Work closely with developers to remediate the vulnerabilities and strengthen the application's security posture.
- Re-Testing and Validation: After remediation, re-test the application to ensure that the identified vulnerabilities have

been effectively resolved. Validate that security measures are now in place.

- Regression Testing: Conduct regression testing to ensure that the security fixes have not introduced new vulnerabilities or affected the application's functionality.
- Documentation: Document the entire security testing process, including the test plan, test cases, test results, identified vulnerabilities, and remediation actions taken.
- Reporting: Generate a comprehensive security testing report that outlines the vulnerabilities discovered, their impact, and recommended actions. This report serves as a guide for developers and stakeholders.
- Review and Approval: Review the security testing report with relevant stakeholders, including developers, testers, and management. Obtain approval for implementing the recommended security measures.
- Continuous Improvement: Integrate security testing into the software development lifecycle as an ongoing practice. Continuously monitor emerging threats, update security testing methodologies, and enhance the security posture.

7.3.1 Conclusion

The security testing process plays a pivotal role in identifying and mitigating vulnerabilities and potential security risks within software applications. By systematically evaluating the application's security measures and addressing vulnerabilities, organizations can ensure the confidentiality, integrity, and availability of sensitive data and functionalities.

CASE STUDY: EFFECTIVE USE OF SECURITY TESTING TECHNIQUES AT SECURETECH CORPORATION

In this case study, we explore how SecureTech Corporation utilized security testing techniques to assess the security of their web application.

Example: SecureTech Corporation conducted regular vulnerability scans using automated tools to identify security weaknesses in their application. They also performed penetration testing to simulate real-world attacks and evaluate the effectiveness of their security measures. Through these efforts, they successfully identified and addressed potential vulnerabilities, ensuring the robustness of their application.

Practical Exercise:

- Perform a security assessment for a software system in your organization. Follow these steps.
- Choose a security testing approach (white-box, black-box, or gray-box) based on the available information and access to the system.
- Select appropriate security testing techniques, such as vulnerability scanning, penetration testing, or code reviews.
- Conduct security tests to identify potential security vulnerabilities and weaknesses.
- Document and prioritize the identified security issues based on their severity and potential impact.
- Collaborate with the development team to implement necessary security measures and address the identified vulnerabilities.

By applying security testing approaches and techniques, you can identify potential security risks and take appropriate measures to mitigate them, ensuring the security of your software system.

7.4 Security Testing Tools

Security testing tools are essential components in identifying vulnerabilities and weaknesses within software applications, networks, and systems. These tools facilitate comprehensive assessment and analysis, enabling organizations to address potential security risks and enhance their overall security posture. Here are some prominent security testing tools.

Burp Suite: Burp Suite is a widely used web vulnerability scanner and security testing tool. It helps identify vulnerabilities such as SQL injection, XSS, and more through automated and manual testing.

OWASP Zed Attack Proxy (ZAP): The OWASP ZAP is an open-source security tool that aids in identifying security vulnerabilities during web application development. It provides automated scanners and features for manual security testing.

Nessus: Nessus is a popular vulnerability assessment tool that scans networks, systems, and applications for known vulnerabilities. It offers comprehensive vulnerability management and reporting capabilities.

Metasploit: Metasploit is a penetration testing tool that helps assess the security of systems by simulating attacks. It provides a wide range of exploits and payloads for various vulnerabilities.

Acunetix: Acunetix is a web vulnerability scanner that detects and reports security issues in web applications. It assists in identifying vulnerabilities such as XSS, SQL injection, and more.

Qualys: Qualys offers cloud-based security and compliance solutions, including vulnerability management and assessment. It helps organizations identify and prioritize vulnerabilities across their infrastructure.

Wireshark: Wireshark is a network protocol analyzer that captures and inspects network traffic. It assists in identifying security threats, suspicious activities, and unauthorized access attempts.

Open Vulnerability Assessment System (OpenVAS): OpenVAS is an open-source vulnerability scanner that assesses networks and systems for known vulnerabilities and misconfigurations.

Nexpose: Nexpose by Rapid7 is a vulnerability management tool that provides insights into security risks, vulnerabilities, and compliance issues across IT environments.

AppScan: IBM Security AppScan helps identify security vulnerabilities in web applications, mobile apps, and APIs. It assists in detecting issues like injection attacks and authentication vulnerabilities.

Netsparker: Netsparker is a web vulnerability scanner that automates the identification of security flaws in web applications. It helps organizations address vulnerabilities proactively.

Veracode: Veracode offers a cloud-based platform for application security testing, including static analysis, dynamic analysis, and software composition analysis.

Snort: Snort is an open-source intrusion detection and prevention system (IDS/IPS) that monitors network traffic for suspicious activities and potential security breaches.

Detectify: Detectify is an automated web security scanner that helps identify vulnerabilities in web applications and provides actionable insights for remediation.

Rapid7 InsightVM: Rapid7 InsightVM offers vulnerability management and assessment capabilities, helping organizations discover and prioritize vulnerabilities.

In conclusion, security testing tools are essential for identifying vulnerabilities, weaknesses, and potential security risks within software applications and systems. By utilizing these tools, organizations can enhance their security measures, address vulnerabilities, and ensure the confidentiality, integrity, and availability of sensitive data and functionalities.

7.5 Security Testing Best Practices

Security testing best practices are essential guidelines that organizations follow to ensure the integrity and security of their software applications. Beginning security testing early in the software development process is a fundamental principle, as it allows vulnerabilities to be identified and addressed before they escalate. A crucial step in this process is threat modeling, where potential attack vectors are assessed and security efforts are prioritized. Employing a variety of security tests, such as vulnerability assessments, penetration testing, and code reviews, helps ensure a comprehensive evaluation of an application's security posture.

Realistic testing is also crucial; simulating real-world attack scenarios helps reveal how attackers might exploit vulnerabilities. Collaboration between development, testing, and security teams is vital to facilitate a proactive approach to security. Secure coding practices should be instilled among developers, emphasizing practices like input validation and secure error handling. Secure configuration of servers, databases, and network components prevents misconfigurations that could expose sensitive data.

Encrypting sensitive data during storage and transmission, implementing strong access controls, and adhering to the principle of least privilege contribute to a robust security foundation. Regular patching and updates are crucial to addressing known vulnerabilities, while thorough scrutiny of third-party components prevents security gaps. Establishing secure development guidelines, offering ongoing security training, and maintaining an incident response plan ensures a holistic security approach.

Embracing these best practices not only mitigates risks but also promotes a culture of security consciousness. Continuous improvement is key; security practices must evolve in response to emerging threats and lessons learned from incidents. Ultimately, adhering to security testing best practices helps organizations safeguard sensitive data, protect against security breaches, and build software applications that can withstand a constantly evolving threat landscape.

7.6 Security Testing Challenges

Security testing, a critical component of modern software development, is not without its challenges. The ever-evolving threat landscape poses a significant hurdle as cyber attackers continuously innovate new techniques to exploit vulnerabilities. Keeping pace with these developments and staying up to date with the latest attack vectors demands constant vigilance. The complexity of modern applications amplifies the testing challenge. Applications often consist of intricate architectures, incorporating various interconnected components, third-party libraries, and APIs. Identifying vulnerabilities across this intricate web requires a deep understanding of the system's inner workings.

A notable challenge is the scarcity of expertise in the field. Security testing necessitates specialized skills, and organizations often struggle to find experienced testers proficient in identifying and mitigating vulnerabilities effectively. Moreover, the delicate balance between security testing and adhering to tight project timelines can be daunting. Conducting thorough security tests takes time, and in a fast-paced development environment, there's a risk of compromising on the quality of testing due to resource constraints.

False positives and negatives pose additional complexities. Security testing tools might generate false positives, leading to unnecessary resource allocation for non-existent vulnerabilities. Conversely, false negatives might result in actual vulnerabilities being missed, potentially exposing the application to threats. Striking a balance between stringent security measures and maintaining optimal application functionality can be intricate, as stringent security measures sometimes unintentionally hinder user experience.

Regression testing, especially after implementing security fixes, can introduce new vulnerabilities or disrupt existing functionalities. Ensuring that security enhancements don't inadvertently compromise other parts of the system requires meticulous attention. Cloud computing and DevOps practices have revolutionized software development but also introduced their own set of security testing challenges. Integrating security seamlessly into these agile practices while maintaining the rapid release cycle necessitates careful planning.

The concept of security-by-design, where security is incorporated from the project's outset, might be a paradigm shift for organizations accustomed to addressing security issues retrospectively. Older systems and legacy applications pose unique challenges due to outdated architecture and potentially scarce documentation, making thorough security testing a formidable task.

Considering the diverse array of devices, browsers, and operating systems on which applications must function, ensuring consistent security across all platforms can be a significant challenge. Continuous monitoring is also critical, as security is an ongoing process. Establishing robust monitoring mechanisms to detect and respond to emerging threats requires substantial resources.

Compliance with data protection regulations and industry standards further complicates security testing efforts. Striving for regulatory compliance while managing other testing challenges demands careful coordination and a thorough understanding of the legal landscape. Lastly, limitations in the visibility provided by security testing tools can lead to potential blind spots, leaving vulnerabilities undetected.

Addressing these challenges demands a multidimensional approach encompassing skilled professionals, advanced tools, robust processes, and a commitment to integrate security seamlessly into all stages of software development. By acknowledging and confronting these challenges head-on, organizations can strengthen their software's security posture and better defend against emerging threats.

7.7 Common Security Vulnerabilities and Mitigation

This section focuses on common security vulnerabilities found in software systems and provides strategies for their mitigation.

7.7.1 Common Security Vulnerabilities

Common security vulnerabilities include injection attacks, XSS, CSRF, insecure direct object references, and security misconfigurations. Understanding these vulnerabilities is crucial for effective security testing.

7.7.2 Mitigation Strategies

Mitigating security vulnerabilities involves implementing security best practices such as input validation, output encoding, proper session management, secure coding practices, and secure configuration management. Additionally, regular security patching and updates should be performed to address known vulnerabilities.

CASE STUDY: SUCCESSFUL MITIGATION OF SECURITY VULNERABILITIES AT PRODIGY SYSTEMS INC.

In this case study, we explore how Prodigy Systems Inc. successfully mitigated security vulnerabilities in their enterprise software.

Example: Prodigy Systems Inc. implemented input validation techniques to prevent injection attacks, employed output encoding to protect against XSS, and implemented CSRF tokens to mitigate CSRF attacks. They also conducted regular security audits and ensured that security patches were applied promptly. These measures significantly reduced the risk of security breaches and protected their sensitive data.

Practical Exercise:

- Identify and mitigate security vulnerabilities in a software system in your organization. Consider the following steps:
- Identify potential security vulnerabilities by analyzing the software system and referring to known vulnerabilities.
- Develop a mitigation plan that includes implementing security best practices and addressing identified vulnerabilities.
- Implement security measures such as input validation, output encoding, secure session management, and secure configuration management.
- Regularly update and patch the software system to address known security vulnerabilities.
- Perform security tests to validate the effectiveness of the implemented security measures and ensure the mitigation of identified vulnerabilities.

By understanding common security vulnerabilities and implementing mitigation strategies, you can enhance the security of your software system and protect it from potential security breaches.

In the security testing chapter, we explored the crucial practice of assessing software applications, systems, and networks for vulnerabilities and potential threats. We learned about various security testing types, ranging from vulnerability assessments to penetration testing, and the significance of integrating security measures from the early stages of development. Through understanding security testing best practices, such as threat modeling, secure coding, and continuous monitoring, we recognized the challenges posed by evolving threats, complex application architectures, and resource constraints. Overall, this chapter emphasized the importance of proactive security measures to safeguard sensitive data, mitigate risks, and enhance the resilience of software systems in the face of ever-evolving cybersecurity challenges.

8

USABILITY TESTING

8.1 Introduction to Usability Testing

Usability testing is a vital process that evaluates the user-friendliness and effectiveness of a software system from the perspective of end users. This chapter introduces usability testing and emphasizes its significance in software quality engineering.

8.1.1 What is Usability Testing?

Usability testing involves the assessment of a software system's ease of use, intuitiveness, and overall user experience. Its primary aim is to identify usability issues and gather valuable feedback from users to enhance the system's design and functionality.

8.1.2 Importance of Usability Testing

Usability testing plays a pivotal role in ensuring user satisfaction, improving user adoption, and reducing user errors. By creating software systems that are intuitive, efficient, and enjoyable to use, usability testing leads to increased user productivity and overall customer satisfaction.

CASE STUDY: SUCCESSFUL USABILITY TESTING IMPLEMENTATION AT NEXUS TECHNOLOGIES

Let's examine how Nexus Technologies integrated usability testing into their software development process to enhance the user experience of their mobile application.

DOI: 10.1201/9781032702049-8

Example: Nexus Technologies Conducted usability tests with representative end users to evaluate the application's navigation, layout, and interaction design. Based on the feedback gathered, they iteratively improved the application's user interface, resulting in increased user engagement and positive user feedback.

8.2 Usability Testing Process

Usability testing is a fundamental step in ensuring that software applications meet user needs and expectations by evaluating their usability, user-friendliness, and overall user experience. This process focuses on identifying usability issues, improving interface design, and creating a user-centered product. Here's an overview of the usability testing process.

- Define Objectives: Clearly define the objectives of usability testing, including what aspects of the application's usability you want to assess and improve.
- Select Participants: Recruit a diverse group of participants who represent the application's target user demographic. Participants should be unfamiliar with the application to provide unbiased feedback.
- Create Test Scenarios: Develop realistic test scenarios that mirror how users would interact with the application. These scenarios should cover various tasks and workflows.
- Design Test Materials: Prepare the necessary materials for the usability test, such as prototypes, wireframes, or the actual application. Ensure that the interface is functional and representative of the final product.
- Conduct the Test: Guide participants through the defined test scenarios while observing their interactions and collecting feedback. Encourage participants to think aloud, sharing their thoughts and feelings during the process.
- Gather Feedback: Document participants' feedback, observations, and insights during the usability test. Capture

both positive experiences and areas of frustration or confusion.

- Analyze Data: Analyze the collected data to identify recurring patterns, common usability issues, and user preferences. Look for pain points, bottlenecks, and areas where users struggle.
- Prioritize Improvements: Prioritize usability issues based on their impact and severity. Address critical issues that hinder user interactions and experience first.
- Design Solutions: Collaborate with designers and developers to devise solutions for the identified usability issues. Implement interface changes, interaction improvements, and workflow enhancements.

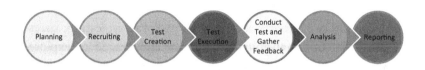

Usability testing process.

- Iterate and Test Again: After implementing the changes, conduct another round of usability testing to validate the effectiveness of the improvements. Iterate this process as needed to achieve optimal usability.
- Document Findings: Compile a comprehensive usability testing report that outlines the identified issues, implemented improvements, and the impact on user experience.
- Feedback Integration: Integrate the usability testing feedback into the software development lifecycle. Use it to inform design decisions, feature enhancements, and ongoing improvements.
- Continuous Iteration: Usability testing is an ongoing process. Continuously gather user feedback, monitor user behavior, and refine the application's usability to meet evolving user expectations.

In conclusion, the usability testing process plays a pivotal role in ensuring that software applications are intuitive, user-friendly, and aligned with user needs. By systematically assessing user interactions and incorporating feedback-driven improvements, organizations can create applications that offer an exceptional user experience and foster user satisfaction.

8.3 Types of Usability Testing

Usability testing encompasses a range of methods aimed at evaluating the user experience of software applications, identifying usability issues, and improving the overall user-friendliness of the product. Different types of usability testing cater to various aspects of user interaction and provide valuable insights. Here are some common types of usability testing.

- Exploratory Usability Testing: In exploratory testing, users are given minimal guidance and are encouraged to explore the application naturally. This type of testing helps uncover unexpected usability issues and provides insights into users' initial impressions.
- Comparative Usability Testing: Comparative testing involves presenting users with multiple versions of the application or different design options. This allows for direct comparison and helps determine which design elements are more intuitive and user-friendly.
- A/B Testing: A/B testing involves presenting users with two different versions of a particular feature or design element. This helps identify which version performs better in terms of user engagement and satisfaction.
- Formative Usability Testing: Formative testing occurs during the design and development process. Users provide feedback on prototypes, wireframes, or early-stage versions of the application, guiding design decisions and improvements.
- Summative Usability Testing: Summative testing takes place after the application is fully developed. It aims to assess the overall usability and user satisfaction with the final product.

- Remote Usability Testing: Remote testing allows users to participate in usability testing from their own locations. This method provides flexibility and a broader reach for gathering user feedback.
- Moderated Usability Testing: Moderated testing involves a facilitator who guides users through test scenarios and observes their interactions in real time. The facilitator can ask follow-up questions to gather deeper insights.
- Unmoderated Usability Testing: Unmoderated testing is conducted independently by users without a facilitator. Users follow predefined scenarios and provide feedback asynchronously.

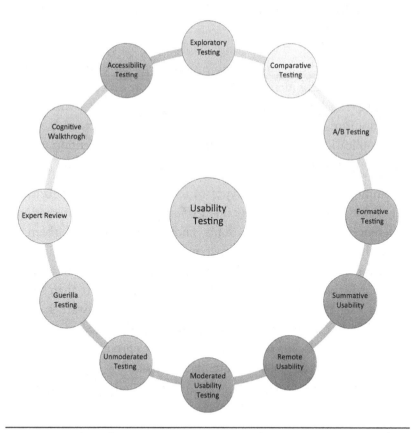

Types of usability testing.

- Guerilla Usability Testing: Guerilla testing involves conducting brief, impromptu usability tests with individuals encountered in public spaces. It provides quick and informal feedback.
- Expert Review (Heuristic Evaluation): In this method, usability experts evaluate the application against a set of usability principles or heuristics. They identify potential usability issues based on their expertise.
- Cognitive Walkthrough: Cognitive walkthroughs simulate user interactions step by step, evaluating the ease of task completion and identifying any cognitive challenges users might face.
- Accessibility Testing: Accessibility testing assesses the application's usability for individuals with disabilities. It ensures compliance with accessibility standards and enhances inclusivity.
- Beta Testing: Beta testing involves releasing a pre-release version of the application to a selected group of users. Their feedback helps identify usability issues before the official launch.
- Eye Tracking Testing: Eye tracking technology is used to monitor users' eye movements as they interact with the application. It provides insights into visual attention and navigation patterns.

By employing these various types of usability testing, organizations can gain a comprehensive understanding of user interactions, preferences, and challenges. This knowledge empowers them to refine the user experience, enhance usability, and create applications that align with users' needs and expectations. "It should be obvious from our list of items to test that usability testing is more than simply seeking user opinions or high-level reactions to a software application. When the errors have been found and corrected, and an application is ready for release or for sale, focus groups can be used to elicit opinions from users or potential purchase."

8.4 Usability Testing Tools: Enhancing User-Centric Design

Usability testing tools are valuable resources that facilitate the evaluation of software applications from a user experience perspective. These tools provide insights into how users interact with the application, helping identify usability issues, improve interface design, and enhance overall user satisfaction. Here are some prominent usability testing

- UserTesting: UserTesting offers a platform for remote usability testing, allowing organizations to gather real-time feedback from users across diverse demographics. It provides video recordings of users' interactions and insights into their thoughts and emotions.
- Crazy Egg: Crazy Egg provides heatmaps, click maps, and scroll maps that visualize how users interact with web pages. These visualizations help identify where users click, scroll, and engage the most.
- Optimal Workshop: Optimal Workshop offers a suite of tools for information architecture and usability testing. It includes tools like Treejack for testing navigation structures and OptimalSort for card sorting exercises.
- UsabilityHub: UsabilityHub offers tools such as Five Second Test, Click Test, and Preference Test to gather quick feedback on designs, interactions, and user preferences.
- Lookback: Lookback enables remote user testing with real-time video streaming of participants' interactions. It also provides features for collaborative analysis and note-taking.
- Loop11: Loop11 offers usability testing and user experience analytics, including remote testing, card sorting, and first click testing.
- UserZoom: UserZoom is a user research platform that offers usability testing, surveys, and user analytics to gather comprehensive insights into user behavior and preferences.
- Morae: Morae by TechSmith provides tools for usability testing, remote testing, and video analysis. It records user interactions and captures their thoughts as they navigate through the application.
- Usabilla: Usabilla offers feedback collection tools that allow users to provide feedback on specific elements within an application, such as buttons, images, and forms.

- Validately: Validately offers tools for remote moderated and unmoderated usability testing, allowing researchers to observe user interactions and gather feedback in real time.
- Maze: Maze is a user testing platform that integrates with design tools to turn prototypes into interactive tests. It offers insights into user interactions, clicks, and navigation paths.
- TryMyUI: TryMyUI provides remote usability testing, where users are given specific tasks to complete while their interactions and feedback are recorded.
- Userlytics: Userlytics offers remote user testing with features such as video recording, surveys, and analytical insights.
- Helio: Helio enables designers and researchers to gather feedback on designs, prototypes, and concepts through visual surveys and interactive user testing.

These usability testing tools empower organizations to gather valuable user feedback, visualize user interactions, and make informed design decisions. By utilizing these tools, organizations can create applications that provide a seamless and user-friendly experience, ultimately enhancing user satisfaction and engagement.

8.5 Usability Testing Methods and Techniques

This section focuses on various methods and techniques used in usability testing to assess the user-friendliness and effectiveness of a software system.

8.5.1 Think-Aloud Testing

Think-aloud testing involves users verbalizing their thoughts and actions while performing specific tasks on the software system. This method provides valuable insights into users' cognitive processes, frustrations, and comprehension of the system's interface.

8.5.2 Task-Based Testing

Task-based testing requires users to perform predefined tasks on the software system while their interactions and performance are observed. This technique helps evaluate the system's usability in real-world scenarios.

8.5.3 Surveys and Questionnaires

Surveys and questionnaires collect subjective feedback from users regarding their satisfaction, ease of use, and overall experience with the software system. They provide both quantitative and qualitative data to assess the system's usability.

8.6 Usability Testing Best Practices

Usability testing best practices form the cornerstone of creating software applications that prioritize user experience and satisfaction. By adhering to these practices, organizations ensure that their products are intuitive, user-friendly, and aligned with user expectations. Clear objectives serve as a foundation for successful testing, outlining precisely what aspects of usability need assessment and improvement. Selecting a diverse group of participants representing the target audience is essential to gather insights from various perspectives. Realistic test scenarios are crafted to simulate real-world interactions, enabling participants to engage authentically with the application.

Central to usability testing is a user-centered approach, where understanding users' needs, behaviors, and preferences takes precedence. Encouraging participants to provide honest feedback in a non-judgmental environment fosters open communication. The think-aloud protocol encourages participants to verbalize their thought processes during interaction, shedding light on decision-making patterns. Unbiased facilitation ensures that participants' interactions remain unaffected by external influence.

Observing both verbal and non-verbal cues offers a comprehensive understanding of participants' experiences. Thorough documentation captures their interactions, feedback, and observations, forming the basis for analysis and improvement. Video recordings provide a visual record of user interactions, enhancing the depth of analysis. The combination of quantitative data, such as task completion rates, and qualitative data, comprising participants' comments, offers a holistic perspective on usability.

Usability testing is an iterative process, integrating feedback-driven improvements at each stage of design and development. Incorporating expert review supplements user insights with heuristic evaluations. Balancing the sample size with diverse perspectives ensures a well-rounded view of usability challenges. Transparent reporting encapsulates findings, usability issues, and proposed solutions, guiding decision-making and collaborative action.

Cross-functional collaboration involving designers, developers, and stakeholders is crucial in reviewing usability testing results and implementing improvements. Usability testing is a continuous journey, emphasizing ongoing user feedback, design refinements, and iterative enhancement. In embracing these usability testing best practices, organizations craft software applications that not only meet user needs but also excel in providing a seamless, enjoyable, and rewarding user experience.

CASE STUDY: EFFECTIVE USE OF USABILITY TESTING METHODS AT TECH SOLUTIONS INC.

Let's explore how **Tech Solutions Inc.** implemented different usability testing methods to improve the user experience of their web application.

Example: Tech Solutions Inc. conducted think-aloud testing sessions with representative users, observed their interactions, and analyzed their feedback to identify usability issues. They also used surveys and questionnaires to gather user opinions and preferences. These insights helped them refine the application's user interface and enhance user satisfaction.

Approach: The company adopted a user-centered approach, starting with participant selection. They recruited a diverse group of participants representing different age groups, tech-savviness levels, and familiarity with the app. The testing was conducted remotely, allowing participants to interact with the app in their own environments.

Test Scenarios: The usability testing scenarios were designed to cover common tasks users performed on the app, such as browsing products, adding items to the cart, and completing the checkout process. The scenarios were intended to simulate real-world usage patterns.

Execution: Participants were provided with access to the app and asked to perform the designated tasks while sharing their thoughts aloud. Video recordings were captured to observe their interactions, facial expressions, and any moments of confusion or frustration. A facilitator observed the sessions remotely, noting participants' comments and insights.

Findings:

- The usability testing sessions uncovered several key findings.
- Participants struggled with the navigation menu, often having difficulty finding specific product categories.
- Some users found the checkout process confusing, resulting in abandoned carts.
- A significant number of participants faced challenges with input fields and form submissions.

Action Plan: Based on the findings, the company devised an action plan.

Navigation Enhancement: The navigation menu was redesigned to make it more intuitive, with clear category labels and icons.

Simplified Checkout: The checkout process was streamlined, and additional guidance was provided at each step.

Form Optimization: Input fields were optimized for mobile devices, and clearer error messages were implemented.

Iterative Testing: After implementing the changes, the company conducted another round of usability testing to validate the improvements. Participants' interactions were smoother, and the usability issues identified earlier were significantly reduced.

Impact:

- The usability testing process led to tangible improvements in the mobile app's user experience: User engagement and conversion rates increased due to the streamlined checkout process.

- The redesigned navigation menu enhanced users' ability to explore and find products.
- The application's overall user-friendliness led to positive user feedback and reviews.

Conclusion:

Through a systematic usability testing approach, the e-commerce company not only identified usability issues but also successfully enhanced the user experience of their mobile app. By prioritizing user needs, addressing pain points, and iteratively testing improvements, they achieved higher user satisfaction, increased engagement, and a stronger competitive edge in the market. This case study exemplifies how usability testing can drive meaningful enhancements that directly impact user interactions and business outcomes.

Practical Exercise:

Perform a usability test for a software system in your organization using the following steps:

- Define specific tasks or scenarios that represent typical user interactions with the software system.
- Select usability testing methods that are appropriate for your objectives and available resources (think-aloud testing, task-based testing, surveys, questionnaires, etc.).
- Recruit representative users who match the target user profile for the software system.
- Conduct usability tests, observe users' interactions, and collect feedback on their experience.
- Analyze the collected data and identify usability issues, pain points, and areas for improvement.
- Implement changes to the software system's design and functionality based on the identified usability issues.
- Repeat the usability testing process to validate the effectiveness of the implemented improvements.

By incorporating usability testing methods and techniques, you can identify and address usability issues, resulting in an improved user experience and increased user satisfaction.

8.7 User Experience Design Principles

This section focuses on essential user experience (UX) design principles that guide the creation of intuitive and user-friendly software systems.

8.7.1 User-Centered Design

User-centered design involves placing the needs and preferences of end users at the forefront of the design process. It emphasizes understanding user goals, tasks, and expectations to create interfaces that align with user needs.

8.7.2 Consistency and Familiarity

Consistency in design elements and interactions promotes ease of use and reduces user confusion. Familiarity with commonly used design patterns and conventions enhances user intuition and accelerates learning.

8.7.3 Visual Hierarchy and Information Architecture

Establishing a clear visual hierarchy and organizing information effectively improves the system's usability. Users should be able to locate and access information effortlessly based on its importance and relevance.

CASE STUDY: SUCCESSFUL IMPLEMENTATION OF USER EXPERIENCE DESIGN PRINCIPLES AT MEGA GLOBE SOLUTIONS

Let's explore how Mega Globe Solutions applied user experience design principles to create a user-friendly and visually appealing e-commerce platform.

Example: Mega Globe Solutions ensured consistency in design elements and navigation across different sections of their platform. They used clear visual hierarchy techniques, such as appropriate use of typography, color, and spacing, to guide users' attention and improve information comprehension. By incorporating user feedback, they refined the platform's information architecture to enhance usability and user satisfaction.

Practical Exercise:

Apply user experience design principles to a software system in your organization using the following steps:

- Identify the target users and their goals and tasks when using the software system.
- Analyze the existing design and interface elements for consistency and alignment with user expectations.
- Refine the visual hierarchy by adjusting typography, colors, spacing, and layout to guide users' attention effectively.
- Evaluate and optimize the system's information architecture to ensure ease of navigation and information access.
- Gather feedback from users on the updated design and incorporate their suggestions and preferences.

By incorporating user experience design principles, you can create software systems that are intuitive, visually appealing, and optimized for user satisfaction.

9

CONTINUOUS INTEGRATION AND CONTINUOUS TESTING

9.1 Introduction to Continuous Integration (CI)/ Continuous Testing (CT)

CI and CT are essential practices in software development that aim to ensure the quality and stability of software systems throughout their lifecycle. This chapter introduces CI/CT and highlights their significance in software quality engineering.

9.1.1 What are CI and CT?

CI is the process of regularly merging code changes from multiple developers into a shared repository. It involves automatically building and testing the software system to identify integration issues and ensure that the codebase remains working.

CT, on the other hand, is the practice of executing automated tests continuously throughout the development process. It helps identify defects, regression issues, and compatibility problems early on, ensuring that the software system meets the desired quality standards.

9.1.2 Importance of CI/CT

CI/CT facilitates faster feedback loops, early defect detection, and improved collaboration among development and testing teams. By integrating and testing code continuously, organizations can catch issues early, reduce the cost of fixing defects, and deliver software systems that are reliable, stable, and of high quality. Here's a step-by-step breakdown of the CI workflow.

DOI: 10.1201/9781032702049-9

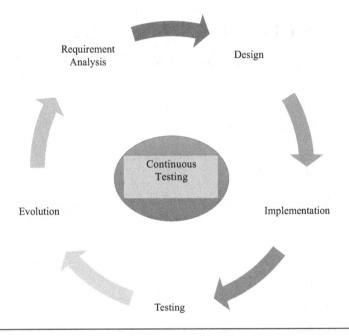

Continuous testing process.

- Code Development: Developers work on individual features, bug fixes, or enhancements in their respective branches of the version control system.
- Code Commit: Once a developer completes their changes, they commit the code to the version control repository, accompanied by meaningful commit messages.
- Automated Build: Upon each code commit, an automated build process is triggered. This process compiles the code, resolves dependencies, and generates a build artifact.
- Code Integration: The build artifact is then integrated into a shared integration branch, often referred to as the "main" or "develop" branch.
- Automated Testing: A suite of automated tests is executed on the integrated codebase. This suite includes unit tests,

integration tests, and possibly other types of tests relevant to the application.

- Test Results: The results of the automated tests are generated, indicating whether the code changes passed all tests or if any issues were detected.
- Reporting: The CI system generates detailed reports about the build process, test outcomes, and any identified issues.
- Feedback Loop: If the automated tests reveal any failures or issues, the development team is notified immediately through the CI system.
- Issue Resolution: Developers work to address any issues identified in the automated tests, aiming to ensure that the codebase remains functional and reliable.
- Code Review: Before merging code changes into the integration branch, a peer review or code review process may take place to ensure code quality and adherence to coding standards.
- CI Server: A dedicated CI server (e.g., Jenkins, Travis CI, Circle CI) orchestrates the entire workflow. It monitors code commits, initiates build, executes tests, and generates reports.
- Iteration: The CI workflow repeats whenever code changes are committed. Developers continue to work on their tasks, commit code, trigger builds, and ensure the integration branch remains stable.

9.1.3 Benefits

The CI workflow offers numerous benefits, including:

- Early Issue Detection: Automated tests catch issues early in the development cycle, reducing the effort required for debugging later.
- Frequent Integration: Frequent code integration minimizes integration risks, making it easier to identify and resolve conflicts.

- Consistent Code Quality: Regular testing enforces code quality standards, enhancing the reliability of the software.
- Collaboration: The shared integration branch encourages collaboration, as developers can work on features simultaneously without disrupting each other.
- Rapid Feedback: Immediate notifications of test results enable rapid feedback, allowing developers to address issues promptly.

In summary, the CI workflow plays a pivotal role in modern software development by promoting collaboration, code quality, and early issue detection. By integrating code changes frequently and automatically validating them through automated testing, development teams can streamline their processes, improve software quality, and deliver more reliable applications.

CASE STUDY: SUCCESSFUL IMPLEMENTATION OF CI/CT AT TECH SOLUTIONS INC.

Let's examine how Tech Solutions Inc. implemented CI/CT practices to enhance its software development process and improve overall product quality.

Example: Tech Solutions Inc. utilized a CI system to automatically build and test their software after every code commit. They implemented an extensive suite of automated tests, including unit tests, integration tests, and system tests, which provide rapid feedback on code changes.

By dealing with issues early and ensuring the stability of their software system, they were able to deliver products with higher quality and a faster time to market.

9.2 Building a CT Pipeline

This section focuses on the process of building a CT pipeline, which involves automating the execution of various types of tests throughout the software development lifecycle.

9.2.1 Test Selection and Prioritization

To build an efficient CT pipeline, it is important to select and prioritize tests based on their relevance, coverage, and execution time. This helps optimize testing efforts and provides faster feedback on critical functionalities.

9.2.2 Test Automation

Test automation plays a crucial role in CT. Automated tests should be developed using frameworks and tools that allow for easy execution and integration into the CI/CT pipeline. This enables efficient and reliable execution of tests on each code committed.

9.2.3 Test Orchestration and Reporting

Test orchestration involves managing the execution of tests in a coordinated manner, ensuring dependencies and prerequisites are met. Additionally, comprehensive reporting and result analysis enable quick identification and resolution of issues.

CASE STUDY: EFFECTIVE CT PIPELINE AT VISIONTECH ENTERPRISES

Let's explore how VisionTech Enterprises established a CT pipeline to streamline its testing efforts and improve overall software quality.

Example: VisionTech Enterprises integrated its test suite into its CI system, allowing tests to be automatically executed after each code commit. They prioritized their tests based on critical functionalities and executed them in parallel to reduce testing time. Test results were collected, analyzed, and reported to relevant stakeholders, enabling timely resolution of issues and ensuring a stable software system.

Practical Exercise:

Build a CT pipeline for a software system in your organization using the following steps:

1. Identify and prioritize the relevant tests based on critical functionalities and areas of high risk.
2. Select appropriate test automation frameworks and tools that integrate seamlessly with your CI system.
3. Automate the execution of tests, including unit tests, integration tests, and regression tests.
4. Establish a test orchestration mechanism to manage dependencies and ensure efficient test execution.
5. Implement a comprehensive reporting mechanism that provides actionable insights for issue resolution.

By building a robust CT pipeline, you can achieve faster feedback on code changes, detect defects early, and deliver software systems of higher quality.

9.3 Test Environment and Data Management

This section focuses on managing test environments and test data to ensure the effectiveness and reproducibility of CT.

9.3.1 Test Environment Provisioning

It is crucial to establish a reliable and consistent test environment that closely resembles the production environment. This involves creating virtualized or containerized environments that can be easily provisioned and replicated.

9.3.2 Test Data Management

Test data plays a significant role in ensuring comprehensive test coverage. Managing test data involves creating representative datasets, automating the generation and manipulation of data, and ensuring data privacy and security.

CASE STUDY: EFFECTIVE TEST ENVIRONMENT AND DATA MANAGEMENT AT GLOBAL REACH SOLUTIONS

Let's explore how **Global Reach Solutions** established a robust test environment and data management practices to support its CT efforts.

Example: Global Reach Solutions utilized infrastructure-as-code techniques to automate the provisioning of test environments. They employed data generation and anonymization tools to create diverse and realistic test datasets while ensuring compliance with data privacy regulations. This enabled them to perform thorough and reliable testing while maintaining data integrity and security.

9.4 Challenges and Best Practices For CI/CT

This section addresses the challenges commonly encountered in implementing CI/CT practices and provides best practices to overcome them.

9.4.1 Overcoming Integration Issues

Integration issues may arise due to conflicting code changes from multiple developers. Employing version control systems, conducting regular code reviews, and establishing clear integration guidelines help mitigate integration challenges.

9.4.2 Managing Test Execution Time

As the test suite grows, managing test execution time becomes critical. Prioritizing tests, parallelizing test execution, and leveraging distributed testing environments can help optimize test execution time.

9.4.3 Ensuring Test Reliability

Test reliability is crucial for accurate results. Regular maintenance of test scripts, monitoring the stability of test environments, and performing periodic checks on test infrastructure ensure test reliability.

9.4.4 Collaboration and Communication

Collaboration between development, testing, and operations teams is essential for successful CI/CT implementation. Encouraging cross-functional collaboration, establishing clear communication channels, and fostering a culture of shared responsibility promote effective CI/CT practices.

CASE STUDY: OVERCOMING CHALLENGES AND IMPLEMENTING BEST PRACTICES AT SYNERGY SOLUTIONS LTD.

Let's examine how Synergy Solutions Ltd. addressed common challenges in implementing CI/CT practices and adopted best practices to ensure their success.

Example: Synergy Solutions Ltd. implemented strict code review processes and utilized CI tools to detect and resolve integration issues promptly. They optimized their test suite by prioritizing tests based on risk and executing them in parallel using distributed testing environments. Regular maintenance of test scripts and environments, along with effective communication between teams, enabled them to overcome challenges and realize the benefits of CI/CT.

Practical Exercise:

Implement CI/CT practices in your organization, considering the following best practices:

- Establish clear guidelines for code integration and conduct regular code reviews to mitigate integration issues.
- Prioritize and parallelize tests to optimize test execution time.
- Regularly maintain and update test scripts and test environments to ensure test reliability.

- Encourage collaboration and communication between development, testing, and operations teams.

9.5 CI Tools

CI tools are essential components of modern software development, automating the integration, testing, and deployment processes. These tools streamline collaboration, enhance code quality, and ensure that code changes are integrated smoothly into a shared repository. Here's a selection of popular CI tools used by development teams.

- Jenkins: Jenkins is an open-source CI/CD tool that enables developers to automate build, test, and deployment processes. Its extensibility through plugins and wide community support makes it a versatile choice for various project requirements.
- Travis CI: Travis CI is a cloud-based CI service designed to work seamlessly with GitHub repositories. It automatically triggers builds on code changes and supports multiple programming languages and frameworks.
- Circle CI: Circle CI provides cloud-based CI/CD services with easy configuration using YAML files. It supports parallelism, caching, and customizable workflows, facilitating efficient testing and deployment pipelines.
- GitLab CI/CD: Integrated within GitLab, GitLab CI/CD offers a complete CI/CD platform. It supports automatic testing and deployment upon code changes and is tightly integrated with GitLab's version control and issue-tracking features.
- TeamCity: TeamCity by JetBrains is a CI server with robust features and support for various languages and platforms. It offers comprehensive build configurations, build chains, and integrations with popular tools.
- Bamboo: Bamboo by Atlassian is a CI/CD server that integrates well with other Atlassian products like Jira and Bitbucket. It provides flexibility in defining build and deployment plans.

- GitHub Actions: GitHub Actions, integrated within GitHub, automates workflows based on code events. It offers a wide range of predefined actions and enables custom scripting for tailored CI/CD pipelines.
- GitLab Runner: GitLab Runner is a component of GitLab CI/CD that allows running builds on various platforms. It supports Docker, Kubernetes, and other virtualization technologies.
- Jenkins X: Jenkins X extends Jenkins for Kubernetes-based applications. It automates CI/CD for cloud-native projects and integrates with container registries and Kubernetes clusters.
- Build kite: Build kite is a CI/CD platform that focuses on customizable pipelines. It supports building, testing, and deploying code across different environments.
- Code ship: Code ship provides cloud-based CI/CD services with straightforward setup using YAML configuration files. It supports parallelism and offers integration with container services.
- Semaphore: Semaphore offers cloud-based CI/CD services with a user-friendly interface and straightforward pipeline setup. It supports parallelism and integrates with popular version control systems.
- Bitrise: Bitrise is a CI/CD platform specifically designed for mobile app development. It offers pre-configured workflows for iOS and Android projects.
- Jenkins Pipelines: Jenkins Pipelines is an extensible suite of plugins that enable building complex, scripted CI/CD pipelines as code, stored alongside application source code.
- Drone: Drone is an open-source CI/CD platform that focuses on simplicity and ease of use. It supports defining pipelines using a.drone.yml configuration file.

These CI tools empower development teams to automate code integration, testing, and deployment processes, enhancing collaboration, code quality, and software delivery efficiency. The choice of tool depends on project requirements, technology stack, and the team's preferred workflows.

9.6 CT Strategies

CT is an integral aspect of modern software development that ensures rigorous testing practices are seamlessly integrated into the Agile workflow. It focuses on automating testing processes, providing rapid feedback, and maintaining high code quality throughout the development lifecycle. Here are several effective CT strategies that development teams can adopt.

Automated Unit Testing: Automated unit tests validate individual units or components of code, ensuring they function as intended. Developers write unit tests for each code change, and these tests are executed automatically during the CI process. These tests catch basic functionality issues early in the development cycle.

Integration Testing: Integration tests assess the interactions between different components, modules, or services of an application. They verify that integrated parts work together as expected. Automated integration tests help identify compatibility issues and unexpected behavior arising from component interactions.

Functional Testing: Functional tests validate the overall functionality of the application by testing its features and user interactions. Automated functional tests simulate user actions and ensure that the application meets user requirements.

Regression Testing: Regression tests verify that new code changes do not break existing functionality. Automated regression tests are executed frequently, preventing the reintroduction of previously fixed bugs.

Performance Testing: Performance tests assess an application's responsiveness, scalability, and stability under various load conditions. Automated performance tests help detect performance bottlenecks and ensure optimal application performance.

Security Testing: Security tests assess an application's vulnerability to security threats. Automated security tests help identify potential security weaknesses and ensure that security measures are in place.

Usability Testing: Usability tests evaluate the user-friendliness and user experience of the application. Automated usability tests can assess aspects such as navigation, interface design, and user interactions.

Continuous Exploratory Testing: Exploratory testing involves manual testing by skilled testers who explore the application and discover defects creatively. Integrating exploratory testing into the CT process allows testers to provide valuable insights.

Cross-Browser and Cross-Platform Testing: Automated tests should cover different browsers, devices, and platforms to ensure consistent functionality across a variety of environments.

Test Data Management: Effective test data management ensures that automated tests have access to relevant and realistic data. Automated tools can help manage test data provisioning.

Parallel and Distributed Testing: Running tests in parallel or across distributed environments increases testing speed and efficiency. Automated test execution across different environments can uncover compatibility issues.

Continuous Monitoring: Continuous monitoring tools track the application's health, performance, and user experience in production. Monitoring helps detect issues after deployment and ensures that the application remains reliable.

Test Automation Frameworks: Adopting test automation frameworks streamlines test creation, execution, and maintenance. Frameworks provide standardized structures and libraries for efficient test development.

Collaborative Testing: Encourage collaboration between developers, testers, and other stakeholders. Shared ownership of testing encourages a holistic approach to quality.

Feedback Loop Improvement: Continuously analyze test results and feedback to identify areas for improvement in the testing process. This iterative approach enhances the effectiveness of CT.

By implementing these CT strategies, development teams can ensure that their applications are thoroughly tested, defects are detected early, and high-quality software is delivered consistently. This approach not only accelerates development cycles but also enhances customer satisfaction and enables organizations to respond rapidly to changing market demands.

By addressing challenges and implementing best practices, you can achieve successful CI/CT implementation, leading to improved software quality and faster delivery cycles.

In the next chapter, we will explore the field of Requirements Engineering and its significance in software quality engineering.

10

REQUIREMENTS ENGINEERING AND QUALITY

10.1 Role of Requirements Engineering in Quality

In the journey towards impeccable software quality, the crucial role of requirements engineering shines through. This chapter delves into the realm of effective requirements engineering practices and their significant impact on software systems' overall quality.

10.1.1 Understanding Requirements Engineering

Requirements engineering is the art of eliciting, analyzing, documenting, and validating software requirements. At its core, it establishes a clear understanding of stakeholders' needs, providing a solid foundation for software design, development, and testing.

10.1.2 Importance of Requirements Engineering in Quality

A clear and well-defined set of requirements forms the bedrock of high-quality software. By eliminating ambiguity, aligning stakeholder expectations, and enabling effective testing and validation, robust requirements engineering paves the way for improved software quality and heightened customer satisfaction.

CASE STUDY: IMPACT OF REQUIREMENTS ENGINEERING ON QUALITY AT PRIME TECH SOLUTIONS

Take a closer look at how Prime Tech Solutions harnessed strong requirements engineering practices to elevate their software quality.

DOI: 10.1201/9781032702049-10

Example: Prime Tech Solutions invested significant time and effort in precisely understanding and documenting customer requirements. Collaborating closely with stakeholders, they employed various techniques like interviews, workshops, and prototypes for validation and conducted meticulous requirements reviews. This approach ensured that the development team possessed a crystal-clear vision of the desired system functionality, culminating in high-quality software that exceeded customer expectations.

10.2 Eliciting and Validating Requirements

This section ~~delves~~ into the art of effectively eliciting and validating software requirements, crucial steps in the pursuit of quality.

10.2.1 Eliciting Requirements

The art of eliciting requirements involves gathering information from stakeholders to gain deep insights into their needs and expectations. Techniques like interviews, surveys, workshops, and observation come into play to elicit requirements comprehensively.

10.2.2 Validating Requirements

To ensure completeness, consistency, and alignment with stakeholder expectations, validating requirements holds immense importance.

Reviews, prototypes, and simulations are valuable techniques utilized to validate requirements against quality criteria.

CASE STUDY: EFFECTIVE ELICITATION AND VALIDATION OF REQUIREMENTS AT PRODIGY SYSTEMS INC.

Discover how Prodigy Systems Inc. achieved software quality by skillfully eliciting and validating requirements.

Example: Prodigy Systems Inc. conducted insightful interviews and workshops with stakeholders, masterfully eliciting requirements. Employing prototypes and mock-ups, they meticulously validated requirements and solicited feedback to refine and validate documented requirements. This iterative approach to elicitation and validation empowered them to capture accurate and actionable requirements, laying the foundation for high-quality software.

10.3 Requirement Analysis and Prioritization

Once requirements have been gathered, the process of analysis and prioritization begins. This crucial phase involves carefully reviewing and understanding the collected requirements, refining them as needed, and assigning priority levels to ensure that the most important features are addressed effectively.

10.3.1 Understanding Requirements

- Thoroughly reviewing and comprehending each requirement.
- Clarifying ambiguities, resolving inconsistencies, and validating their feasibility.

10.3.2 Refining Requirements

- Breaking down high-level requirements into smaller, manageable tasks.
- Ensuring that requirements are clear, specific, and well-defined.

10.3.3 Tracing and Linking

- Establishing traceability between requirements and other development artifacts, such as design and test cases.
- Ensuring that each requirement can be traced back to its origin and associated changes.

10.3.4 Prioritizing Requirements

- Categorizing requirements based on their business value, technical feasibility, and impact on the project's goals.
- Assigning priority levels (e.g., high, medium, low) to guide development and testing efforts.

10.3.5 MoSCoW Method

- Using the MoSCoW method (Must-have, Should-have, Could-have, Won't-have) to prioritize requirements.
- Identifying critical features that are essential for the core functionality (Must-haves) and distinguishing optional enhancements (Should-haves and Could-haves).

10.3.6 Kano Model

- Applying the Kano model to categorize requirements based on their impact on user satisfaction.
- Distinguishing between basic expectations, performance features, and delighters that exceed user expectations.

10.3.7 Risk Analysis

- Assessing the risks associated with different requirements.
- Prioritizing requirements that mitigate high-risk factors or address critical project constraints.

10.3.8 Stakeholder Involvement

- Engaging stakeholders in the prioritization process to align requirements with business needs.
- Balancing different perspectives and priorities from various stakeholders.

10.3.9 Collaboration and Communication

- Ensuring clear communication between the development team, business stakeholders, and users.
- Collaboratively deciding on the final prioritization based on shared understanding.

10.3.10 Agile Prioritization Techniques

- Implementing agile techniques like backlog grooming and sprint planning to adjust priorities iteratively.
- Ensuring that priorities are aligned with the evolving needs of the project.

10.3.11 Documentation and Communication

- Documenting the prioritized requirements in a clear and accessible format.
- Sharing the priorities with the development team and stakeholders for alignment.

10.3.12 Managing Changes

- Recognizing that priorities may change as the project progresses.
- Adapting to new information, changing business needs, and evolving market conditions.

10.3.13 Balancing Trade-offs

- Acknowledging that prioritization involves trade-offs between conflicting requirements.
- Making informed decisions based on project constraints and stakeholder input.

Effective requirements analysis and prioritization ensure that development efforts are focused on delivering the most valuable features and functionalities to users. It helps avoid scope creep, aligns development with business goals, and ultimately leads to the successful delivery of high-quality software that meets user expectations.

10.4 Requirements Engineering Challenges

The process of requirements engineering is not without its challenges. Addressing these challenges is essential to ensure the successful delivery of high-quality software that meets users' needs and business objectives.

10.4.1 Incomplete Requirements

- Gathering complete and accurate requirements can be challenging due to evolving user needs or unclear project goals.
- Strategies: Engage in continuous communication with stakeholders, conduct a thorough analysis, and use iterative development to refine requirements over time.

10.4.2 Ambiguous or Unclear Requirements

- Vague or poorly defined requirements can lead to misunderstandings and misinterpretations.
- Strategies: Use clear and precise language, create visual aids like diagrams, and involve stakeholders in reviews to achieve a shared understanding.

10.4.3 Changing Requirements

- The dynamic nature of software projects often results in changing requirements, leading to scope creep.
- Strategies: Implement change management processes, prioritize changes based on business value, and communicate changes effectively to all stakeholders.

10.4.4 Conflicting Requirements

- Different stakeholders may have conflicting expectations or priorities for the software.
- Strategies: Facilitate open communication among stakeholders, involve them in prioritization, and seek consensus when resolving conflicts.

10.4.5 Unrealistic Expectations

- Setting unrealistic expectations for project timelines or features can lead to dissatisfaction.
- Strategies: Set clear expectations with stakeholders, involve them in estimation, and provide transparent updates on project progress.

10.4.6 Scope Creep

- Unauthorized additions or changes to requirements during the project can affect timelines and budgets.
- Strategies: Use change control processes, document changes thoroughly, and educate stakeholders about the impact of scope changes.

10.4.7 Requirements Volatility

- Rapidly changing requirements can result in instability and increased development effort.
- Strategies: Implement agile practices, focus on iterative development, and ensure flexibility to accommodate evolving requirements.

10.4.8 Lack of User Involvement

- Insufficient engagement with end-users can lead to requirements that don't align with user needs.
- Strategies: Establish regular feedback loops, involve users in requirements reviews, and conduct user acceptance testing.

10.4.9 Poor Communication

- Miscommunication between stakeholders and development teams can lead to misaligned expectations.
- Strategies: Foster transparent and effective communication channels, document decisions, and conduct regular status updates.

10.4.10 Technological Challenges

- Complex technology or unfamiliar domains can make it difficult to capture accurate requirements. "If the program does not meet the requirements, or does not operate normally (e.g., crashes randomly, does not respond to user input, etc.), then a defect has been found" [9].
- Strategies: Involve domain experts, conduct feasibility studies, and use prototypes to clarify technical aspects.

10.4.11 Lack of Requirements Traceability

- Failing to establish traceability between requirements and other project artifacts can lead to inconsistencies.
- Strategies: Use tools to maintain traceability matrices, ensure proper documentation, and track changes across the project.

10.4.12 Cultural and Organizational Challenges

- Different organizational cultures and structures can affect the requirements gathering and validation process.
- Strategies: Foster cross-functional collaboration, address cultural differences, and ensure alignment with organizational goals.

Addressing these challenges requires a proactive approach, effective communication, collaboration among stakeholders, and the use of appropriate tools and methodologies. By recognizing and mitigating these challenges, software development teams can ensure that their requirements engineering process leads to successful project outcomes.

10.5 Requirements Traceability and Management

This section unravels the significance of requirement traceability and management in the pursuit of software quality.

10.5.1 Requirements Traceability

Requirements traceability establishes a robust link between requirements and various artifacts in the software development lifecycle, such as design documents, test cases, and code. This ensures that all requirements are diligently addressed and validated throughout the development process.

10.5.2 Requirements Management

Effective requirements management involves capturing, documenting, and organizing requirements. This includes version control, change management, maintaining a comprehensive requirements repository, fostering collaboration, and ensuring that requirements remain up to date.

CASE STUDY: SUCCESSFUL REQUIREMENTS TRACEABILITY AND MANAGEMENT AT QUANTUM INNOVATIONS

Explore how Quantum Innovations championed requirement traceability and management to nurture exceptional software quality.

Example: Quantum Innovations leveraged a top-notch requirements management tool, meticulously tracking the traceability of requirements throughout the development process. With a well-defined change control process in place, they adeptly managed requirement changes, keeping all stakeholders informed and involved. This holistic approach to requirement traceability and management facilitated the integrity of requirements, ultimately resulting in top-notch software quality.

Practical Exercise:

Elevate requirements engineering practices in your organization with the following steps:

- Embrace a rich variety of techniques, such as interviews, workshops, and prototypes, to masterfully elicit requirements from stakeholders.
- Validate requirements through insightful reviews, prototypes, and simulations to ensure their completeness and consistency.

11

CODE QUALITY AND STATIC ANALYSIS

11.1 Introduction to Code Quality

Embarking on the quest for excellence, code quality emerges as a linchpin in software development, shaping the software systems' reliability, maintainability, and overall quality. This chapter embarks on an exploration of code quality, illuminating its profound significance in software quality engineering.

11.1.1 Understanding Code Quality

Code quality embodies the measure of effectiveness, efficiency, and adherence to coding standards in software code. A hallmark of high-quality code is its readability, maintainability, and robustness, with a sound foundation in good design principles and best coding practices.

11.1.2 Importance of Code Quality

Code quality's impact resonates across various facets of software development, from the software system's reliability and performance to its ease of maintenance and the ability to embrace new features and modifications. Well-structured and clean code improves the overall quality of software, mitigating the risk of defects and software failures.

CASE STUDY: IMPROVING CODE QUALITY AT STARCOM ENTERPRISES

Uncover the journey of StarCom Enterprises as they endeavored to elevate their software reliability and maintainability through improved code quality.

DOI: 10.1201/9781032702049-11

Example: StarCom Enterprises instituted a thorough code review process, placing emphasis on code readability, maintainability, and adherence to coding standards. Regular code reviews became the norm, with constructive feedback offered to developers, ensuring that code changes were rigorously reviewed before integration. By making code quality a priority, they remarkably reduced defects and elevated the overall quality of their software.

11.2 Static Analysis Tools and Techniques

This section unveils the power of static analysis tools and techniques in assessing and enhancing code quality.

11.2.1 Introduction to Static Analysis

Static analysis entails scrutinizing code without executing it and uncovering potential defects, vulnerabilities, and violations of coding standards. By automating this process, static analysis tools become invaluable, providing essential insights into code quality.

11.2.2 Benefits of Static Analysis

The wonders of static analysis are far-reaching, enabling early identification of coding errors, security vulnerabilities, performance bottlenecks, and other code quality issues. With static analysis tools at their disposal, development teams proactively address these issues, elevating the overall quality of their code.

CASE STUDY: EFFECTIVE USE OF STATIC ANALYSIS TOOLS AT STARCOM ENTERPRISES

Embark on the journey of ABC Corporation, harnessing static analysis tools to bolster code quality and reduce software defects.

Example: StarCom Enterprises seamlessly integrated static analysis tools into their development process, seamlessly incorporating them into their continuous integration pipeline. Configured to enforce coding standards and identify potential defects and security vulnerabilities, these tools empowered them to proactively address code quality issues, leading to a significant reduction in software defects.

11.3 Code Review and Inspection

This section shines a spotlight on the art of code review and inspection as a formidable weapon to fortify code quality.

11.3.1 Importance of Code Review

Code review entails a methodical examination of code by peers or senior developers, a potent way to unearth defects, ensure adherence to coding standards, and offer feedback for improvement. Code review's impact is profound, enhancing code quality, fostering knowledge sharing, and nurturing collaboration among team members.

11.3.2 Static Analysis Tools

SonarQube: SonarQube is a widely used static analysis platform that checks code for quality, security, and maintainability issues. It provides detailed reports, identifies code smells, and offers integration with various programming languages.

- Checkstyle: Checkstyle is a static analysis tool that enforces coding standards for Java code. It identifies violations of style and formatting rules, ensuring consistency and maintainability.
- PMD: PMD is a source code analyzer for Java, JavaScript, and other languages. It detects code issues, such as unused variables, inefficient code, and potential bugs.
- ESLint: ESLint is a popular static analysis tool for JavaScript. It checks code against best practices, identifies coding errors, and enforces coding style guidelines.
- Find Bugs: Find Bugs is a static analysis tool for Java that identifies potential bugs and defects in code. It highlights issues related to correctness, performance, and security.

- Cppcheck: Cppcheck is a static analysis tool for C and C++ code. It detects coding errors, memory leaks, and other potential issues in the codebase.
- Bandit: Bandit is a security-focused static analysis tool for Python code. It scans code for security vulnerabilities, such as potential SQL injection and XSS vulnerabilities.
- Infer: Infer is a static analysis tool developed by Facebook that focuses on identifying potential defects, crashes, and performance issues in mobile app codebases.
- Coverity: Coverity is a comprehensive static analysis tool that detects defects, vulnerabilities, and security weaknesses in a wide range of programming languages.
- Klocwork: Klocwork is a static analysis tool that supports various languages and identifies coding defects, security vulnerabilities, and performance issues.
- CodeSonar: CodeSonar is a sophisticated static analysis tool that identifies complex coding defects, security vulnerabilities, and potential violations of industry standards.
- Fortify: Fortify is a static analysis tool by Micro Focus that focuses on security vulnerabilities in code. It offers vulnerability assessment and prioritization.
- Coveralls: Coveralls is a code coverage and static analysis tool that helps measure code coverage and identify untested parts of the codebase.
- JSHint: JSHint is a static analysis tool for JavaScript that identifies potential coding issues, enforces best practices, and ensures code quality.
- Snyk: Snyk is a security-focused static analysis tool that scans code for open-source vulnerabilities and provides insights into potential security risks.

These static analysis tools offer developers and teams valuable insights into their code quality, security, and compliance with coding standards. By integrating static analysis into the development process, organizations can proactively identify and address issues, leading to more robust, secure, and maintainable software applications.

11.3.3 Code Inspection Techniques

In the pursuit of exceptional code quality, code inspection techniques emerge as essential. These techniques encompass a meticulous examination of code to identify common code quality issues, such as coding errors, suboptimal design choices, and performance bottlenecks. Manual code review, walkthroughs, and pair programming stand as effective code inspection techniques. "The longer a defect stays in the system and goes undetected, the greater the impact. It also is true that leaving bugs festering in a code base has a negative effect on code quality, system intuitiveness, system flexibility, team morale, and velocity" [10].

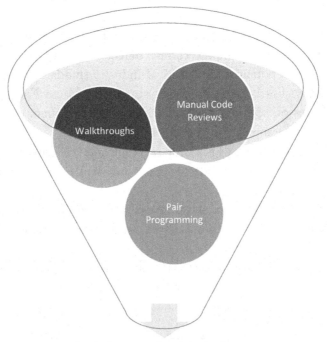

Code Inspection Techniques

Code inspection techniques.

CASE STUDY: SUCCESSFUL CODE REVIEW PRACTICES AT STELLAR SOLUTIONS INC.

Witness the prowess of Stellar Solutions Inc. as they embrace code review practices, elevate code quality, and nurture a culture of collaboration.

Example: Stellar Solutions Inc. implemented a stellar code review process, subjecting every code change to thorough review by peers. By emphasizing coding standards, design principles, and potential defects during review, this process led to exceptional code quality, promoted knowledge sharing, and ensured consistent coding practices across the team.

Practical Exercise:

Soar to new heights of code quality in your development projects with these steps:

- Integrate static analysis tools into your development process, arming yourself with the insights to identify and address code quality issues early.
- Establish a code review process, ensuring that code changes undergo meticulous review by peers or senior developers.
- Leverage code inspection techniques, such as manual code review or pair programming, to uncover common code quality issues and offer feedback for improvement.

By championing code quality and making use of static analysis tools and code review practices, you will herald a new era of software systems defined by exceptional quality, reliability, and maintainability.

12

DEFECT MANAGEMENT AND ROOT CAUSE ANALYSIS

12.1 Defect Life Cycle and Management

In the intricate realm of software development, defects are bound to emerge. Effectively managing these issues becomes paramount to ensuring software quality. This chapter delves into the defect life cycle and unveils diverse techniques for adept defect management.

12.1.1 Defect Life Cycle

The journey of a defect from identification to resolution encompasses crucial stages like defect logging, triaging, prioritization, assignment, fixing, retesting, and closure. Each stage plays a pivotal role in the quest for impeccable software quality.

12.1.2 Benefits Of Effective Defect Management

Effective defect management is a crucial practice in software development that involves identifying, tracking, prioritizing, and resolving defects or issues within the software codebase. This process has far-reaching benefits that contribute to improved software quality, streamlined development cycles, and overall project success. Here are some key advantages of implementing effective defect management.

- Improved Software Quality: Efficient defect management ensures that identified issues are resolved promptly before they reach users. This leads to a higher-quality software product with fewer bugs, glitches, and user-reported problems.
- Enhanced Customer Satisfaction: By addressing defects before they impact users, organizations deliver a more reliable and user-friendly product. This directly translates to

DOI: 10.1201/9781032702049-12

increased customer satisfaction, positive user experiences, and improved brand reputation.

- Faster Issue Resolution: Effective defect management involves clear documentation, prioritization, and assignment of issues to appropriate team members. This streamlines the resolution process, leading to faster fixes and reduced downtime.

- Predictable Development Cycles: Defect management provides insights into the state of the software at any given time. This allows for better planning, estimation, and predictability of development cycles, reducing the likelihood of unexpected delays.

- Reduced Rework Costs: Addressing defects early in the development process minimizes the need for extensive rework. This not only saves time but also reduces the costs associated with fixing issues after they have propagated through the codebase.

- Efficient Resource Allocation: Defect management helps teams allocate resources efficiently by prioritizing and assigning defects based on severity and impact. This ensures that critical issues receive immediate attention.

- Enhanced Collaboration: Defect management tools and processes facilitate collaboration between developers, testers, and other stakeholders. Clear communication about defects and their status promotes teamwork and shared ownership of quality.

- Continuous Improvement: The analysis of defect patterns and root causes allows organizations to identify systemic issues in their development processes. This insight fosters continuous improvement, leading to fewer defects over time.

- Better Decision-Making: Defect management provides data-driven insights into the quality of the software. These insights aid project managers and stakeholders in making informed decisions about release readiness and project direction.

- Risk Mitigation: Effectively managing defects helps organizations identify and address potential risks before they escalate into critical issues. This minimizes the impact of unexpected problems on project timelines and goals.

- Improved Documentation: Defect management requires thorough documentation of issues, their resolution steps, and associated information. This documentation becomes a valuable resource for future reference and knowledge sharing.

- Compliance and Audit Readiness: In regulated industries, effective defect management ensures that software complies with standards and regulations. Proper documentation of defect resolution can demonstrate adherence to compliance requirements during audits.

In conclusion, effective defect management plays a pivotal role in achieving software excellence, project success, and customer satisfaction. By promptly identifying, addressing, and learning from defects, organizations can deliver higher-quality products, reduce development cycles, and create a more efficient and collaborative development environment.

12.1.3 Importance of Defect Management

Through the lens of effective defect management, teams can efficiently track and resolve defects, delivering high-quality software to end-users. Moreover, it offers invaluable insights to identify patterns, enhance processes, and prevent similar issues from recurring.

CASE STUDY: STREAMLINING DEFECT MANAGEMENT AT TECH SOLUTIONS INC.

Embark on the journey of Tech Solutions Inc. as they refine their defect management process to elevate software quality and enhance team efficiency.

Example: Tech Solutions Inc. implemented a centralized defect tracking system that allowed seamless logging, tracking, and prioritization of defects. The clear definition of roles and responsibilities for defect management, along with well-established guidelines for resolution and closure, further contributed to their success. Streamlining the defect management process resulted in reduced resolution time and an overall improvement in software quality.

12.2 Defect Tracking Tools and Processes

Effectively managing defects is greatly enhanced by the strategic utilization of defect tracking tools and processes. This section uncovers their significance in the grand scheme of things.

12.2.1 Defect Tracking Tools

Defect tracking tools act as a centralized repository, streamlining the process of logging, tracking, and managing defects. With features like priority assignment, progress tracking, document attachments, and report generation, these tools pave the way for effective defect management. Defect tracking tools are also known as issue tracking tools and are essential software applications that facilitate the identification, monitoring, and resolution of defects, bugs, and issues within a software development project. These tools play a crucial role in maintaining software quality, fostering collaboration, and ensuring efficient project management. Here are several widely used defect tracking tools and their features.

- Jira: Jira, developed by Atlassian, is one of the most popular issue tracking tools. It offers customizable workflows, user story mapping, and comprehensive reporting. Jira supports agile methodologies, enabling teams to manage defects alongside user stories, tasks, and epics.
- Bugzilla: Bugzilla is an open-source defect tracking tool that provides a simple interface for issue management. It offers customizable fields, advanced search capabilities, and integration with version control systems.
- Trello: Trello is a visually oriented project management tool that can be adapted for defect tracking. Its card-based system enables teams to create cards for defects, assign them, and track their progress on a Kanban-style board.
- Redmine: Redmine is an open-source issue tracking tool that supports multiple projects, custom fields, and role-based access control. It offers integration with version control systems and features like time tracking and Gantt charts.
- Asana: Asana is a versatile project management tool that can be used for defect tracking. It offers task management,

collaboration features, and customizable boards that teams can use to track and prioritize issues.

- YouTrack: YouTrack, developed by JetBrains, is a robust issue tracking tool that supports agile methodologies and offers features like custom workflows, intelligent search, and detailed reporting.
- MantisBT: MantisBT is an open-source issue tracking system that is easy to set up and use. It supports customizable fields, email notifications, and role-based access control.
- GitHub Issues: GitHub Issues is integrated with GitHub repositories and offers basic issue tracking features. Teams can create issues, assign them, and link them to code changes and pull requests.
- GitLab Issues: Similar to GitHub Issues, GitLab Issues is integrated within GitLab and provides issue tracking capabilities. It offers seamless integration with GitLab's version control and continuous integration features.
- Microsoft Azure DevOps: Formerly known as Visual Studio Team Services, Azure DevOps provides a comprehensive suite of tools for software development, including issue tracking, version control, continuous integration, and more.
- Zoho BugTracker: Zoho BugTracker is part of the Zoho suite of applications and offers features like issue assignment, custom workflows, and integration with other Zoho products.
- Freshdesk: Although primarily a customer support tool, Freshdesk can be adapted for defect tracking. It allows teams to log, manage, and prioritize issues reported by users.

Defect tracking tools facilitate collaboration among development teams, testers, and stakeholders, ensuring that defects are identified, prioritized, and resolved efficiently. By providing transparency, accountability, and clear communication, these tools contribute to the overall quality and success of software development projects.

12.2.1.1 Defect Tracking Processes   The seamless management of defects hinges on well-defined defect tracking processes. This encompasses capturing detailed defect information, assigning ownership, setting priorities, defining resolution criteria, and continuously monitoring the status of defect resolution. The defect tracking process is a systematic approach used in software development to identify, document, prioritize, and manage defects, bugs, and issues that arise during the development lifecycle. This process plays a pivotal role in maintaining software quality, enhancing collaboration, and delivering a reliable product. Here's a step-by-step breakdown of the defect tracking process.

- Defect Identification: Defect identification begins with stakeholders reporting issues they encounter. These issues could be bugs, unexpected behaviors, or any deviations from desired functionality. Defects can also be identified through automated testing, code reviews, and manual testing processes.
- Issue Documentation: Each identified defect is documented in detail. This documentation includes a description of the issue, steps to reproduce it, screenshots, and any relevant logs or error messages. Thorough documentation ensures that the defect is understood and can be replicated by development and testing teams.
- Defect Categorization and Prioritization: Defects are categorized based on their impact, severity, and the areas of the application they affect. Prioritization involves assigning a priority level (such as high, medium, or low) to each defect, considering factors like the defect's impact on users, functionality, and project timelines.
- Assigning Ownership: Defects are assigned to relevant team members, such as developers or testers, who are responsible for addressing them. Clear ownership ensures that defects are actively worked on and not overlooked.
- Defect Replication and Analysis: Assigned team members replicate the reported defect in their development or test environment. They analyze the code to identify the root cause of the defect. This analysis helps determine whether the issue is indeed a defect and whether it requires fixing.
- Defect Resolution: The development team works on fixing the defect by modifying the codebase. They address the root cause, implement the necessary changes, and thoroughly test the code changes to ensure they do not introduce new issues.

- Verification and Testing: After the defect is resolved, the testing team verifies the fix by retesting the issue in their test environment. They ensure that the issue is resolved and that the fix does not impact other areas of the application.
- Regression Testing: Regression testing involves testing the entire application to ensure that the defect fix did not inadvertently introduce new defects or affect other parts of the software.
- Approval and Deployment: Once the defect fix is verified, it goes through an approval process. Project stakeholders review the fix to ensure that it aligns with project goals. If approved, the fix is deployed to the production environment.
- Closure and Documentation: After the defect is fixed and verified, it is marked as closed in the defect tracking tool. The entire process is documented, including the details of the defect, its resolution, and the steps taken for verification.
- Monitoring and Analysis: Defect tracking data is analyzed to identify patterns, recurring issues, and potential areas for process improvement. This analysis informs continuous improvement efforts.

Effective defect tracking ensures that defects are identified, resolved, and documented in a structured manner, ultimately contributing to a higher-quality software product. The process promotes collaboration, accountability, and a focus on delivering reliable and user-friendly software applications.

CASE STUDY: EFFECTIVE USE OF DEFECT TRACKING TOOLS AT SECURETECH CORPORATION

Dive into the success story of **SecureTech Corporation** as they embrace defect tracking tools to revolutionize their defect management process and elevate software quality.

Example: SecureTech Corporation seamlessly integrated a robust defect tracking tool into their development process. Accompanied by a standardized defect tracking process that encompassed clear guidelines for logging, triaging, and resolution, they were able to manage defects effectively. The automation of the process ensured timely resolution and minimized potential disruptions.

12.3 Root Cause Analysis (RCA) Techniques

RCA emerges as a systematic approach to identifying and addressing the underlying causes of defects. In this section, we explore diverse RCA techniques and their impact on software quality.

12.3.1 Importance of RCA

RCA is the key to unlocking the deeper reasons behind defects, allowing teams to address core issues rather than just treating symptoms. Understanding and addressing root causes paves the way for preventing the recurrence of similar defects in future projects.

12.3.2 RCA Techniques

A repertoire of techniques, such as the 5 Whys, Fishbone diagram, Pareto analysis, and fault tree analysis (FTA), empowers teams to trace the root causes of defects, identify contributing factors, and facilitate effective corrective actions. RCA is a systematic approach used to identify

Fishbone diagram.

the underlying causes of problems, defects, and issues within various processes, systems, or projects. By addressing the root causes, organizations can prevent recurring problems and improve overall efficiency. Here are several effective techniques commonly employed in RCA.

- Fishbone Diagram (Ishikawa Diagram): Also known as a fishbone diagram or Ishikawa diagram, this technique visually represents potential causes of a problem as branches on a "fishbone" structure. It categorizes causes into various factors such as people, processes, equipment, materials, and environment, aiding in identifying the root cause.
- 5 Whys: The 5 Whys technique involves repeatedly asking "why" to delve deeper into the cause of a problem. By asking "why" multiple times, teams can uncover the underlying reasons behind an issue. This technique helps uncover connections and reveals the root cause of the problem.
- Pareto Analysis (80/20 Rule): Pareto analysis involves identifying the most significant contributing factors to a problem. It follows the 80/20 rule, where approximately 80% of the effects come from 20% of the causes. By focusing on the most influential factors, teams can address the root causes effectively.

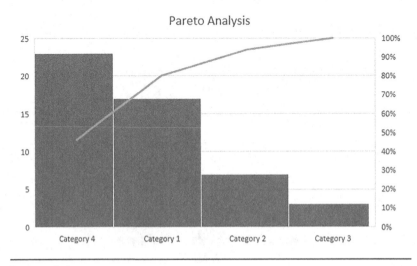

Pareto analysis.

- FTA: FTA is a structured approach that represents the logical relationship between potential causes and their effects on a problem. It provides a visual representation of how failures can occur and helps identify the combination of events that lead to the problem.
- Barrier Analysis: Barrier analysis assesses the factors that should have prevented a problem from occurring. It identifies gaps in the existing barriers, such as policies, procedures, or safeguards, which contributed to the problem's occurrence.
- Failure Mode and Effects Analysis (FMEA): FMEA is a systematic approach that evaluates potential failure modes and their effects. It helps prioritize potential causes based on severity, occurrence, and detection, enabling teams to focus on high-risk root causes.
- Apollo RCA: Developed by NASA, the Apollo technique focuses on identifying potential causes by considering contributing factors related to people, hardware, software, and the environment. It encourages a holistic approach to problem analysis.
- Kepner-Tregoe Problem Analysis: The Kepner-Tregoe technique involves a structured approach to analyzing problems. It guides teams through defining the problem, identifying potential causes, testing hypotheses, and selecting the most likely root cause.
- Change Analysis: Change analysis examines recent changes in processes, systems, or procedures that might have contributed to the occurrence of a problem. It helps identify whether the root cause is related to recent changes.
- DMAIC (Define, Measure, Analyze, Improve, Control): DMAIC is a structured problem-solving framework used in Six Sigma methodology. It guides teams through the steps of defining the problem, measuring current performance, analyzing potential causes, implementing improvements, and establishing control measures.
- Event and Causal Factor Charting (ECFC): ECFC involves charting events and causal factors to understand the sequence of events leading to a problem. It helps identify contributing factors and the chain of events that resulted in the issue.

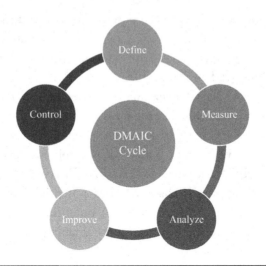

DMAIC cycle.

- Barrier-BowTie Analysis: Similar to FTA, Barrier-BowTie analysis visually represents potential causes, their effects, and the preventive barriers that mitigate risks. It helps identify the weaknesses in existing barriers.

Each RCA technique offers a structured approach to uncovering the underlying causes of issues. The choice of technique depends on the complexity of the problem, the available data, and the preferences of the analysis team. Regardless of the technique used, effective RCA leads to more informed decision-making, improved processes, and enhanced problem-solving capabilities.

CASE STUDY: SUCCESSFUL RCA AT FUTURETECH SERVICES

Step into the shoes of FutureTech Services as they embrace RCA techniques to identify and resolve the underlying causes of defects.

Example: FutureTech Services utilized the 5 Whys technique, relentlessly asking "why" to uncover the deeper layers of defect causality. Complemented by the visual clarity of the Fishbone diagram, they mapped out potential causes and their intricate relationships. This rigorous RCA process resulted in the implementation of effective corrective actions, preventing similar defects from surfacing again.

Practical Exercise:
Elevate defect management in your projects through these steps.

- Integrate a defect tracking tool to establish a centralized repository for logging and tracking defects.
- Define a well-structured defect management process, encompassing guidelines for triaging, assignment, resolution, and closure.
- Embrace RCA techniques to identify and address the underlying reasons behind defects.

"Automating regression tests, running them in an automated build process, and fixing root causes of defects reduces technical debt and permits growth of solid code" [11]. By effectively managing defects and conducting insightful RCA, you can elevate software quality and nurture continuous improvement in your development projects.

13

RELEASE AND DEPLOYMENT MANAGEMENT

13.1 Release Planning and Coordination

Embarking on the journey of software delivery demands adept release and deployment management. In this chapter, we navigate through the intricacies of release planning and coordination to ensure seamless software deployments.

13.1.1 Release Planning

The art of release planning involves meticulous determination of the release scope, timeline, and content. It encompasses activities like setting release goals, defining criteria, prioritizing features, and establishing milestones that ultimately pave the way for successful software releases.

13.1.2 Release Coordination

Release coordination is the thread that weaves together the activities and stakeholders involved in the release process. Through effective coordination, development, testing, and deployment efforts align seamlessly, addressing dependencies and conflicts with precision.

CASE STUDY: STREAMLINING RELEASE MANAGEMENT AT VISIONARY ENTERPRISES LTD.

Uncover the success story of Visionary Enterprises Ltd. as they fine-tuned their release management process, enhancing efficiency and minimizing deployment hurdles.

 DOI: 10.1201/9781032702049-13

Example: Visionary Enterprises Ltd. brought their vision to life by implementing a well-defined release planning process, fostered by collaboration among development, testing, and operations teams. Clear release criteria, identification of potential risks, and contingency plans further fortified their strategy. The result was a streamlined release coordination effort that minimized deployment failures and ensured smooth software rollouts.

13.2 Deployment Strategies and Techniques

In the realm of software deployment, thoughtful consideration of diverse strategies and techniques ensures success and efficiency. This section sheds light on the nuances of deployment strategies and techniques.

13.2.1 Deployment Strategies

The array of deployment strategies includes phased deployment, canary releases, blue–green deployments, and rolling updates. Each strategy comes with its own benefits and considerations, molded by the complexity, size, and criticality of the software at hand.

13.2.2 Deployment Techniques

Deployment techniques transform the chosen deployment strategy into reality. Activities such as configuring deployment environments, packaging software artifacts, managing dependencies, and executing deployment scripts or automation tools collectively orchestrate the process.

Deployment techniques are essential processes in software development that involve delivering software from the development environment to the production environment, where users can access and use the application. These techniques ensure a smooth transition while minimizing disruptions and risks. Here are several common deployment techniques.

- Manual Deployment: In manual deployment, developers or operations teams manually transfer the code, databases, and configurations from the development environment to the production environment. This approach is suitable for smaller projects or when there's a need for precise control over the deployment process.
- Continuous Deployment: Continuous deployment involves automatically deploying every code change to the production environment after passing automated tests and quality checks. This technique is common in Agile and DevOps practices, enabling frequent releases and rapid feedback.
- Continuous Delivery: Continuous delivery focuses on automating the deployment pipeline to ensure that code changes are always ready for deployment but require manual approval before being released to production. This approach strikes a balance between automation and controlled releases.
- Blue–Green Deployment: In a blue–green deployment, two identical environments—blue and green—are set up. The current version of the application (e.g., blue) is in production, while the new version (e.g., green) is deployed alongside it. After testing the green environment, traffic is switched from blue to green, making the new version live.
- Canary Deployment: Canary deployment involves deploying a new version of the application to a small subset of users or servers before a full rollout. This technique allows for testing the new version's performance and stability in a controlled environment.
- Feature Toggles (Feature Flags): Feature toggles enable the activation or deactivation of specific features within the application without deploying new code. This technique allows developers to release features gradually and control their availability to users.
- Rolling Deployment: Rolling deployment involves gradually replacing instances of the old application version with instances of the new version. This is often done in clusters, ensuring that the application remains available during the deployment process.

- Dark Launching: Dark launching involves deploying new features or changes to production but keeping them hidden from users. This allows testing and monitoring of new features without impacting the user experience.
- A/B Testing: A/B testing is a technique where different versions of a feature or UI element are deployed to separate user groups. This allows organizations to gather data on user preferences and make informed decisions based on real-world usage.
- Rollback and Rollforward: Rollback involves reverting to a previous version of the application in case of issues or failures. Rollforward is the opposite, where a failed deployment is corrected and redeployed.
- Immutable Infrastructure: Immutable infrastructure involves deploying new instances of the application instead of updating existing ones. This eliminates configuration drift and ensures consistent environments.
- Serverless Deployment: Serverless deployment involves deploying code as functions or microservices to cloud platforms that automatically manage scaling and infrastructure, relieving developers of deployment-related tasks.
- Each deployment technique offers distinct advantages and is suited for specific scenarios and project requirements. The choice of technique depends on factors such as project.
- "Every time a deployment to production requires an outage, the product is unavailable to your customer. If your product is a website, this may be a huge impact. If your product is an independent product to be downloaded onto a PC, the impact is low. Agile teams release frequently to maximize value to the business, and small releases have a lower risk of a large negative impact. It's common sense to work with the business to time releases for time periods that minimize disruption. Automate and streamline deployment processes as much as possible to keep downtime windows small. A quick deployment process is also helpful during development in short iterations where we may deploy a dozen times in one day" [12].

CASE STUDY: EFFECTIVE DEPLOYMENT TECHNIQUES AT ALPHAOMEGA GROUP

Immerse yourself in the journey of AlphaOmega Group as they embrace effective deployment techniques, ensuring reliable and efficient software deployments.

Example: AlphaOmega Group, mindful of the significance of a phased deployment strategy, gradually rolled out new software versions to specific user groups. Automation tools, such as containerization and infrastructure-as-code, emerged as their allies in the deployment process. The results spoke volumes, as deployment errors dwindled and downtime during releases became a thing of the past.

13.3 Monitoring and Post-Release Activities

An unyielding focus on monitoring and post-release activities forms the crux of evaluating deployment success and addressing any challenges or feedback. This section unearths the power of monitoring techniques and post-release endeavors.

13.3.1 *Monitoring*

In the realm of deployment, monitoring takes center stage, observing the software system in production to ensure stability, performance, and availability. This encompassing task draws on monitoring tools, metric collection, log analysis, and the ability to proactively detect anomalies or performance hiccups.

13.3.2 *Post-Release Activities*

Post-release activities usher in the critical phase of gathering user feedback, analyzing performance data, addressing reported issues, and planning subsequent releases or updates. Through these endeavors, software quality receives continuous enhancement based on user experiences.

13.3.3 Monitoring and Post-Release Activities: Ensuring Software Reliability and Continuous Improvement

Monitoring and post-release activities are critical components of the software development lifecycle that focus on maintaining the performance, reliability, and quality of a deployed application. These activities enable organizations to detect issues, gather insights, and implement improvements to enhance user experiences and meet business objectives. Here's an overview of monitoring and post-release activities.

Monitoring: Effective monitoring involves tracking the application's performance, availability, and user interactions in real time. Monitoring tools and techniques help identify potential issues and ensure that the application is running as expected. Common aspects of monitoring include the following:

- Performance Monitoring: Tracking response times, server load, and resource utilization to ensure optimal performance.
- Availability Monitoring: Monitoring uptime and downtime to promptly address any disruptions.
- Error Monitoring: Detecting errors, exceptions, and crashes in the application to identify and resolve issues quickly.
- User Experience Monitoring: Collecting data on user interactions, navigation patterns, and user satisfaction to improve user experiences.
- Infrastructure Monitoring: Monitoring servers, databases, networks, and other infrastructure components for stability and health.
- Logging and Logging Analysis: Logging involves recording relevant events, activities, and transactions within the application. Analyzing logs helps in identifying trends, patterns, and potential anomalies. Logs provide valuable insights for troubleshooting, debugging, and optimizing the application's performance.
- Incident Response: When issues or incidents occur post-release, organizations should have a well-defined incident response plan in place. This plan outlines the steps to take when a critical issue affects the application's performance or functionality. Incident response aims to minimize downtime, restore service, and communicate with stakeholders effectively.

- Bug Tracking and Defect Resolution: Even after deployment, defects or bugs may emerge as users interact with the application. Organizations should continue tracking and prioritizing these issues, resolving them promptly to maintain a positive user experience.
- User Feedback Analysis: Gathering user feedback and reviews from post-release users is invaluable. Analyzing this feedback provides insights into user perceptions, pain points, and feature requests. This information guides improvements and updates for future releases.
- Performance Optimization: Monitoring data helps identify performance bottlenecks and areas of the application that require optimization. Post-release activities may involve fine-tuning code, optimizing database queries, or implementing caching strategies to improve performance.
- Security Monitoring: Continuously monitoring for security vulnerabilities, threats, and breaches is crucial to safeguard sensitive data. Security monitoring helps identify and address potential risks, ensuring that the application remains secure.
- Patch Management: Software vulnerabilities can be discovered after deployment. Organizations need to proactively address these vulnerabilities by applying patches and updates to keep the application secure and up to date.
- Release Planning and Iteration: Monitoring and post-release activities inform the planning of future releases. Feedback, insights from monitoring, and lessons learned contribute to iterative improvements and the development of new features.
- Continuous Improvement: The insights gained from monitoring and post-release activities contribute to continuous improvement efforts. Organizations can refine their development processes, enhance code quality, and deliver better user experiences based on the knowledge gained from past releases.

By diligently monitoring and conducting post-release activities, organizations can ensure that their software applications remain reliable, performant, and aligned with user needs. These activities also enable organizations to learn from their experiences, enhance their processes, and deliver software that drives user satisfaction and business success.

CASE STUDY: EFFECTIVE MONITORING AND POST-RELEASE ACTIVITIES AT ALPHA CORP INTERNATIONAL

Dive into the success story of Alpha Corp International as they harnessed the power of monitoring and post-release activities to optimize software performance and delight users.

Example: Alpha Corp International equipped themselves with a comprehensive monitoring system that tirelessly watched over their software's performance, availability, and user experience. A feedback mechanism was thoughtfully established to collect user input, and they prioritized addressing reported issues promptly. Active monitoring and post-release engagement became the driving forces behind consistent software quality improvement and soaring user satisfaction.

Practical Exercise:

Elevate your release and deployment management process by embracing these steps.

- Forge a structured release planning process, vividly defining release goals, criteria, and milestones.
- Coordinate effectively with the diverse teams involved in the release process, ensuring seamless communication and alignment.
- Implement the most suitable deployment strategies and techniques tailored to your software's unique characteristics.
- Establish monitoring mechanisms to proactively detect and address issues post-deployment.
- Conduct thorough post-release activities, leveraging user feedback to drive continuous software enhancement.

By weaving effective release and deployment management practices into your software development endeavors, you ensure seamless software rollouts and delight your users with an elevated software experience.

14

INTRODUCTION TO DEVOPS

DevOps, a harmonious blend of collaboration, communication, and integration between development and operations teams, emerges as the focus of this chapter. We explore the essence of DevOps and its intertwining relationship with software quality engineering.

14.1 The Essence of DevOps

The essence of DevOps lies in a set of practices, principles, and cultural values aimed at fostering collaboration and integration between software development (Dev) and IT operations (Ops) teams. The term "DevOps" is a combination of the words "Development" and "Operations," emphasizing the need to bridge the gap between these traditionally separate functions to achieve faster, more reliable software delivery and a better user experience.

14.1.1 DevOps Principles

Continuous integration, continuous delivery, infrastructure automation, and feedback loops guide this principle. DevOps stands as a transformative approach to elevating software development and delivery processes. The outcome? Improved software quality and accelerated time-to-market.

14.1.2 Benefits of DevOps

The DevOps approach bequeaths numerous benefits to the world of software development, including heightened agility, enhanced collaboration, faster time-to-market, and a substantial reduction in deployment failures. By bridging the gap between development and operations teams, DevOps fosters seamless coordination and ensures smoother software delivery.

172

DOI: 10.1201/9781032702049-14

CASE STUDY: IMPLEMENTING DEVOPS AT EXPLORE THE JOURNEY OF SECURETECH CORPORATION AS THEY ADOPTED DEVOPS PRACTICES, STRIVING TO AMPLIFY SOFTWARE QUALITY AND ELEVATE DELIVERY EFFICIENCY

Example: SecureTech Corporation embraced DevOps by weaving together their development and operations teams, employing automation tools for streamlined infrastructure provisioning and deployment. The formation of cross-functional teams responsible for end-to-end software development and delivery set the stage for faster feedback cycles and a culture of continuous improvement.

14.2 Integration of Quality Engineering in DevOps

Integrating quality engineering practices into the heart of DevOps becomes a pivotal aspect of ensuring software quality throughout the development and deployment processes. This section sheds light on the seamless integration of quality engineering in DevOps.

14.2.1 Quality Assurance in DevOps

Quality assurance (QA) is the linchpin of DevOps, playing a pivotal role in guaranteeing that software not only meets but surpasses established quality benchmarks. Its influence extends across the entire software development lifecycle, seamlessly integrating into every phase from initial test planning and meticulous test case design to the rigorous execution of tests and vigilant defect management. This comprehensive integration of QA activities into the intricate tapestry of development and deployment processes serves as a driving force, propelling software quality to unprecedented heights. As a fundamental element of DevOps, QA ensures the consistent delivery of high-quality software, fostering a culture of excellence and reliability in the dynamic landscape of software development.

Kate Falanga, in her role as a Director of Quality Assurance, speaks about formal knowledge sharing between teams to create connections between disciplines. She emphasizes that these sessions are two-way: "I've had people from different kinds of groups in our organization speak at our team meetings. I want to know what [they] do and I want to know how [they] want to interact with us. Having that shared roadshow of speaking at different team meetings is very helpful" [13].

14.2.2 Collaboration and Communication

The essence of DevOps thrives on effective collaboration and communication among development, operations, and quality engineering teams. This virtuous circle empowers quality engineers to provide early feedback, identify potential risks, and define quality metrics for perpetual improvement.

CASE STUDY: QUALITY ENGINEERING INTEGRATION IN DEVOPS AT FUTURETECH SERVICES EMBARK ON THE JOURNEY OF FUTURETECH SERVICES AS THEY SEAMLESSLY INTEGRATE QUALITY ENGINEERING PRACTICES INTO THEIR DEVOPS PHILOSOPHY

Example: FutureTech Services embarked on a "shift-left" approach, introducing quality engineering activities early in the development process. Quality engineers collaborated closely with developers, crafting test cases, and implementing test automation to detect defects at the earliest stages. The result was a seamless feedback loop, enabling early defect detection and faster delivery of quality software.

14.3 Continuous Testing in a DevOps Environment

Continuous testing emerges as the backbone of DevOps, tirelessly validating software throughout the development and deployment pipeline. This section uncovers the nuances of continuous testing in a DevOps environment.

14.3.1 *Test Automation*

At the heart of continuous testing lies test automation, which empowers teams to gain quick insights into software quality, validate changes made during development, and gain unwavering confidence in software stability.

14.3.2 *Test Orchestration and Integration*

Test orchestration and integration pave the way for the harmonious alignment of diverse tests across the DevOps pipeline. Embracing unit tests, integration tests, regression tests, and performance tests, this seamless orchestration ensures tests are executed consistently and efficiently.

CASE STUDY: IMPLEMENTING CONTINUOUS TESTING IN DEVOPS AT DEF CORPORATION

Dive into the journey of QuantumLeap Innovations as they embraced continuous testing practices, ensuring reliability, and efficiency in software deployments.

Example: QuantumLeap Innovations gracefully weaved test automation frameworks and tools into their DevOps pipeline, enabling continuous testing at every stage. They automated unit tests, integration tests, and performance tests, with the results automatically reported and analyzed. Through the power of continuous testing, QuantumLeap Innovations elevated software quality, reduced the risk of defects, and accelerated software delivery.

Practical Exercise:

Infuse quality engineering into your DevOps journey with these steps:

- Foster seamless collaboration among development, operations, and quality engineering teams.
- Implement test automation frameworks and tools to empower continuous testing.

- Establish quality metrics and feedback loops to drive perpetual improvement.
- Streamline the test orchestration process, ensuring efficient test execution throughout the DevOps pipeline.

By integrating quality engineering into your DevOps philosophy, you will experience swifter and more reliable software delivery while maintaining the highest standards of software quality.

15

THE FUTURE OF SOFTWARE QUALITY ENGINEERING

15.1 Artificial Intelligence (AI) and Machine Learning (ML)
Applications in Quality Engineering: Driving Software
Quality and Efficiency

AI and ML have revolutionized numerous industries, including software quality engineering. In this chapter, we delve into the exciting applications of AI and ML in quality engineering and explore how these technologies can improve software quality and testing efficiency.

The advent of AI and ML has introduced transformative capabilities that go beyond traditional testing approaches. AI-powered testing tools can analyze vast amounts of data, identify patterns, and make intelligent predictions, streamlining the testing process and enhancing its accuracy. ML algorithms can also optimize test case selection and execution, leading to more efficient and effective test coverage.

15.1.1 Defect Prediction and Prevention

AI and ML techniques offer the ability to analyze historical data and uncover patterns that correlate with software defects. By harnessing these patterns, quality engineers can predict potential defects and take proactive measures to prevent them, ultimately leading to enhanced software quality.

With the accumulation of historical data from past software development and testing processes, AI and ML algorithms can identify factors that contribute to the occurrence of defects. These factors might include code complexity, module interdependencies, developer experience, and testing coverage. By analyzing these patterns, AI can predict the likelihood of defects in the current

DOI: 10.1201/9781032702049-15

development cycle or in specific parts of the software. Defect prediction empowers quality engineers to focus their efforts on the most vulnerable areas of the codebase, allowing them to allocate resources more efficiently and prioritize testing activities accordingly.

15.1.2 *Test Optimization and Prioritization*

By integrating AI and ML algorithms, quality engineers can optimize and prioritize test cases based on factors such as code changes, risk assessment, and historical defect data. This intelligent approach allows for more efficient test execution while maintaining comprehensive test coverage. "At a high level, software testing is a way of providing an estimate of software quality to stakeholders (that is, people who have a direct interest in the system, such as customers, users, and managers). While stakeholders may not directly care about the quality of software, they are interested in managing risk" [14].

Traditionally, test case selection and prioritization have been manual and based on the tester's judgment. However, with the power of AI and ML, software quality engineering can now leverage data-driven decision-making to enhance testing efficiency. AI algorithms can analyze code changes and identify areas where updates are more likely to affect. By focusing on these critical areas, testing efforts become more targeted and relevant. Risk assessment is another crucial aspect that AI and ML can assist with. These algorithms can evaluate the potential impact of code changes on different parts of the software, helping quality engineers allocate resources based on the level of risk associated with each component. This way, high-risk areas receive more attention, ensuring that the most critical functionalities are thoroughly tested.

CASE STUDY: ENHANCING QUALITY AT RELIABLE SYSTEMS LTD. THROUGH DEFECT PREDICTION

We examine how Reliable Systems Ltd. implemented AI and ML for defect prediction, resulting in improved software quality and fewer defects in production. By utilizing historical defect data and ML algorithms, a defect prediction model was built, enabling focused testing efforts on critical areas prone to defects. The result was a significant reduction in post-release defects.

15.2 Test Automation and AI/ML

Test automation and AI/ML integration have become powerful combinations in the realm of software quality engineering. As the complexity of software applications continues to grow, traditional testing methods often struggle to keep pace with the increasing demands for faster and more reliable testing processes. This is where the integration of AI and ML technologies steps in to revolutionize test automation.

One of the significant advantages of AI/ML in test automation lies in test case generation. While manual test case creation can be time-consuming and error-prone, AI-driven test generation tools can automatically generate a vast number of test cases covering different scenarios and edge cases. This automated test case generation helps achieve broader test coverage, ensuring that various aspects of the software are thoroughly examined for potential defects.

Furthermore, AI/ML technologies can significantly enhance test execution processes. By continuously learning from test results and real-time feedback, AI-powered test automation tools can intelligently prioritize test cases. This adaptive approach focuses testing efforts on critical areas where defects are most likely to occur, thereby optimizing test execution time and resources.

15.2.1 Intelligent Test Generation

By integrating AI and ML algorithms into the testing process, test case generation can be significantly improved. These intelligent technologies can analyze requirements, code, and even user behavior to automatically create a diverse set of test cases. This automation not only speeds up the testing process but also ensures broader test coverage, addressing various usage scenarios and edge cases that may not have been considered in manual test case creation. AI and ML algorithms excel at detecting patterns and anomalies in data. In the context of testing, this capability becomes invaluable for defect detection. These algorithms can identify potential defects or areas of concern that traditional testing methods might have overlooked by analyzing test results and application behavior. As a result, quality engineers can focus their attention on addressing critical issues, leading to more robust and reliable software.

15.2.2 Smart Test Execution and Analysis

Smart test execution and analysis, powered by AI and ML, enhance software testing significantly. It automates test result analysis by examining logs and metrics, providing valuable insights. AI algorithms detect patterns and anomalies in test outcomes, improving defect detection and resolution. These advancements lead to more efficient testing processes and higher software quality.

CASE STUDY: STREAMLINING TESTING AT VISIONTECH ENTERPRISES THROUGH AI-DRIVEN AUTOMATION

We examine how VisionTech Enterprises integrated AI and ML into their test automation process, leading to faster and more effective testing. AI-driven test generation techniques automatically generate test cases, while ML-based analysis tools detect patterns in test results, resulting in faster execution and improved defect detection rates.

15.3 Challenges and Opportunities in AI/ML for Quality Engineering

The dynamic field of AI and ML presents quality engineering with vast opportunities, but these opportunities are not without their share of challenges. As quality engineers embark on harnessing the potential of AI and ML, they must be prepared to address the intricacies and complexities that lie ahead.

Opportunities in AI and ML: The integration of AI and ML technologies in quality engineering holds incredible promise. These advanced technologies can elevate software testing and development to unprecedented heights, leading to enhanced efficiency, accuracy, and overall performance. By embracing AI and ML, quality engineers can unlock the power to streamline processes, identify critical defects, and optimize the user experience.

Challenges in AI and ML: Despite the exciting potential, quality engineering faces certain hurdles when diving into the realm of AI and ML. One of the primary challenges revolves around the need for meticulous planning and consideration. Implementing these cutting-edge technologies demands a comprehensive understanding of the tools, methodologies, and algorithms involved.

Moreover, AI and ML models require vast amounts of high-quality data for training, testing, and validation. Ensuring the availability of such data can be a significant obstacle for quality engineers, as it directly impacts the reliability and effectiveness of AI-driven solutions. Interpreting and understanding the decisions made by AI and ML models is another critical challenge. Building trust with stakeholders hinges on the ability to explain how these models arrive at specific conclusions. The lack of transparency can lead to skepticism and reluctance to adopt AI and ML solutions.

Furthermore, quality engineers must grapple with the ethical considerations surrounding AI and ML implementations. Addressing issues related to privacy, security, and fairness becomes essential to ensuring that these technologies are leveraged responsibly.

15.3.1 Data Quality and Bias

At the heart of successful AI and ML endeavors lies the crucial foundation of data quality. For these cutting-edge technologies to deliver accurate predictions and dependable results, they hunger for a steady diet of high-quality and unbiased data. As quality engineers embark on their quest for excellence, they must meticulously curate and groom datasets, ensuring that they are devoid of any biases that might taint the models' judgments.

In this data-driven era, the adage "garbage in, garbage out" resonates more profoundly than ever. The quality of the input data directly influences the caliber of the output from AI and ML models. By feeding these virtual minds with data that is replete with noise, inconsistencies, or partiality, we are unwittingly setting them up for failure. To fortify their foundation, we must equip these models with data of the utmost integrity and authenticity. However, the path to data quality is not always smooth. Quality engineers often find themselves grappling with issues such as missing data, outliers, and discrepancies. But, armed with determination and the right tools, they venture forth in pursuit of pristine datasets. These dedicated professionals employ data cleaning, data validation, and data normalization techniques to bring order to chaos and purity to noise.

A critical facet of data quality is addressing the lurking specter of bias. Biases can stealthily infiltrate datasets, skewing the AI and ML models' perspectives and insights. These biases can stem from historical data, human judgment, or the data collection process itself. For quality engineers, it is imperative to remain vigilant and proactive in detecting and mitigating biases to ensure that the models remain impartial and fair.

To ensure accurate predictions and reliable results, AI and ML models require high-quality and unbiased data.

15.3.2 Interpretability and Explainability

As AI and ML models rise to prominence and infiltrate various industries, the spotlight shines ever brighter on the critical aspects of interpretability and explain ability. The ability to peel back the layers of these virtual minds and shed light on their decision-making process becomes paramount in fostering trust and confidence among stakeholders.

In the realm of quality engineering, where precision and reliability reign supreme, transparency is no mere luxury; it is an absolute necessity. Stakeholders, be they customers, managers, or regulatory bodies, demand to comprehend the inner workings of AI and ML models. They seek reassurance that these enigmatic algorithms are not wielding their influence arbitrarily or in a black-box fashion.

Interpretability, the capability to decipher and comprehend the rationale behind the models' outputs, empowers quality engineers to gain deeper insights into the strengths and limitations of AI-driven solutions. When faced with an anomaly or an unexpected result, interpretable models allow engineers to traverse the decision-making trail, understand the contributing factors, and make informed decisions on how to proceed.

Explain ability, on the other hand, transcends the realm of comprehension into the realm of communication. It involves articulating the AI and ML models' decisions in a clear, coherent, and intelligible manner, devoid of technical jargon and inscrutable complexities. A skilled quality engineer adept at explaining these models can bridge the chasm between the virtual world and the human domain, making the AI's conclusions understandable and actionable for all stakeholders.

The importance of interpretability and explain ability spans far beyond the confines of the quality engineering domain. Industries where AI and ML applications wield significant influence, such as healthcare, finance, and autonomous vehicles, are acutely aware of the repercussions of opaque decision-making. In these critical fields, misinterpreting or misunderstanding AI outputs could lead to serious consequences, both human and financial.

Addressing the challenges of interpretability and explain ability necessitates a multifaceted approach. Quality engineers can opt for inherently interpretable models, such as decision trees or linear regression, which provide explicit rules for decision-making. Alternatively, post hoc techniques, like LIME (Local Interpretable Model-Agnostic Explanations) or SHAP (Shapley Additive Explanations), offer ways to explain the predictions of complex models. The ability to interpret and explain AI and ML models' decisions is crucial for building trust with stakeholders.

15.3.3 Continuous Learning and Adaptation

In the ever-evolving landscape of software and testing environments, the ability of AI and ML models to embrace continuous learning and adaptation stands as a pivotal attribute. These cutting-edge technologies, akin to virtual chameleons, must possess the agility to transform and evolve in response to the dynamic challenges presented by the fast-paced world of technology.

The concept of continuous learning transcends the traditional paradigm of stagnant models and fixed algorithms. Instead, it heralds a paradigm shift where AI and ML models can acquire new knowledge, refine their understanding, and seamlessly integrate fresh data. AI and ML models capable of absorbing new information and refining their decision-making prowess support and thrive in quality engineering, a discipline grounded in improvement and optimization. In the realm of software and testing environments, change is not only a constant but an accelerating force. New features, updates, and bug fixes are deployed with increasing frequency, demanding AI and ML models to stay current and responsive. The ability to ingest these transformations and adjust their strategies accordingly empowers these models to maintain their effectiveness and relevance over time.

Continuous learning also aligns harmoniously with the concept of adaptability, as both form a symbiotic relationship that nurtures the resilience of AI and ML models. Adaptability endows these virtual entities with the capacity to react to unforeseen scenarios, novel challenges, and unexpected perturbations with poise and flexibility. Like seasoned warriors, they adjust their tactics, recalibrate their approaches, and emerge stronger and wiser from each encounter.

For quality engineers, fostering continuous learning and adaptability in AI and ML models represents both an opportunity and a challenge. The opportunity lies in harnessing the potential of these technologies to elevate testing and quality assurance to unprecedented levels of efficiency and accuracy. By integrating self-improvement mechanisms into the models' architecture, engineers can amplify their capabilities and efficiency manifold.

On the other hand, the challenge lies in designing and implementing these mechanisms effectively. Ensuring that the models do not fall prey to overfitting, forgetting, or becoming overwhelmed by irrelevant information necessitates a delicate balance between retaining past knowledge and being receptive to fresh insights. AI and ML models must be capable of learning and adapting to changing software and testing environments.

15.3.4 Ethical Considerations in AI and ML

As the realm of AI and ML continues to advance and weave itself into the fabric of our daily lives, the significance of addressing ethical concerns looms ever larger. The responsible implementation of these cutting-edge technologies demands a conscientious examination of the potential ramifications for privacy, security, and fairness.

Privacy stands as a cornerstone of individual autonomy and data protection. With AI and ML systems amassing vast amounts of personal information, the need to safeguard this data against unauthorized access and misuse becomes paramount. Quality engineers, developers, and policymakers must collaborate to design robust privacy measures that shield sensitive data from prying eyes and potential breaches, upholding individuals' rights to confidentiality.

Security, akin to an impenetrable fortress, guards against the malevolent forces of cyber threats. AI and ML systems, bolstered by their data-driven decision-making capabilities, are powerful assets. However, they must not become unwitting vectors for malicious intent. Implementing robust security protocols, encryption, and threat detection mechanisms ensures that these technologies become forces for good rather than tools of exploitation.

Fairness, a fundamental tenet of a just society, assumes even greater significance in the realm of AI and ML. These technologies should never perpetuate or exacerbate existing biases or discriminatory practices. Quality engineers bear the responsibility of scrutinizing the algorithms and data used to train these systems, rooting out any traces of prejudice or favoritism, and striving for a level playing field where all individuals are treated equitably. The journey towards addressing ethical considerations in AI and ML requires multidimensional collaboration. It transcends technical expertise, reaching into the realms of philosophy, law, and the social sciences. Ethicists, legal experts, and diverse stakeholders must join forces with AI researchers and developers to forge a path that champions the principles of privacy, security, and fairness. The ethical implications of AI and ML also resonate beyond individual projects and extend into broader societal contexts. Policymakers must navigate the labyrinth of legislation and regulation, striking a balance that fosters innovation while safeguarding against potential harm. Industry standards and Ethical guidelines further reinforce the importance of ethical considerations in the development and deployment of AI and ML technologies. Implementing AI and ML requires addressing ethical concerns related to privacy, security, and fairness.

Opportunity: Leveraging AI/ML for Anomaly Detection: An exciting opportunity in quality engineering is utilizing AI and ML techniques for anomaly detection. This approach allows quality engineers to detect and address potential issues before they impact users, enhancing overall software quality.

Practical Exercise: By following these steps, you can explore the application of AI and ML in quality engineering:

- Identify a quality engineering process or challenge suitable for AI and ML applications, such as defect prediction or test optimization.
- Collect relevant data and assess its quality and potential biases.
- Select appropriate AI and ML algorithms or tools that align with the identified application.
- Implement and validate the AI/ML solution in a controlled environment, monitoring its performance and accuracy.

16

THE SIGNIFICANCE OF QUALITY
METRICS

16.1 The Significance of Quality Metrics in Software Quality Engineering

In the ever-evolving landscape of software development, the quest for excellence has become inseparable from the diligent pursuit of measurable outcomes. Quality metrics, the compass that guides software quality engineering, play a pivotal role in this journey of continuous improvement. This chapter emphasizes the importance of quality metrics in software quality engineering and their role in making informed decisions.

16.1.1 Measuring Software Quality

Quality metrics provide quantitative assessments of software quality, covering dimensions such as reliability, performance, security, and usability. They offer valuable insights into the effectiveness of quality engineering practices and areas that require improvement.

16.1.2 Decision-Making and Risk Management

Metrics supply essential information for decision-making and risk management, enabling stakeholders to prioritize quality improvement efforts and allocate resources effectively based on objective data.

16.1.3 Benefits of Quality Metrics and Analytics

- Informed Decision-Making: Data-backed insights enable stakeholders to make well-informed decisions about project direction, resource allocation, and risk management.

DOI: 10.1201/9781032702049-16

- Early Issue Detection: By monitoring key metrics, organizations can detect issues early in the development lifecycle, preventing them from escalating into major problems.
- Continuous Improvement: Quality analytics promotes a culture of continuous improvement by highlighting areas for optimization, process refinement, and skill development.
- Enhanced Communication: Quantifiable metrics provide a common language for communication among cross-functional teams, ensuring alignment and shared goals.
- User-Centric Development: Metrics related to user satisfaction and feedback guide development efforts toward creating user-centered software.
- Risk Mitigation: Analyzing quality metrics helps identify potential risks and vulnerabilities, allowing proactive measures to be taken to mitigate them.

16.2 Metrics for Software Quality Engineering

In the quest for software excellence, quality engineering relies on a comprehensive set of metrics that serve as the pillars of evaluation and progress. This section sheds light on the key metrics employed in software quality engineering, offering a glimpse into the vital measurements that enable quality engineers to gauge and optimize software quality.

16.2.1 Defect Metrics

Defect metrics form a vital subset of software quality engineering metrics, focusing specifically on the assessment of defects and their impact on software quality. By delving into the realm of defects, quality engineers can gain deeper insights into the software's health, identify potential areas for improvement, and fortify their pursuit of excellence. Defect metrics measure the number, severity, and rate of defects identified during different phases of the software development lifecycle. Examples include defect density, defect arrival rate, and defect removal efficiency.

16.2.2 Test Metrics

In the multifaceted domain of software quality engineering, test metrics form an integral and illuminating aspect. These metrics act as torchbearers, guiding quality engineers through the labyrinth of testing efforts and shedding light on the efficacy and efficiency of the testing process. By delving into the world of test metrics, we gain invaluable insights into the software's robustness, the thoroughness of testing efforts, and the overall health of the quality assurance landscape.

The significance of test metrics cannot be overstated. As quality engineers navigate the complex terrain of software testing, they rely on these metrics to gauge the success of their endeavors. Through meticulous data collection and analysis, these metrics provide a quantitative and objective assessment of the testing process, allowing for informed decision-making and the fine-tuning of testing strategies. Test metrics evaluate the effectiveness and efficiency of testing efforts, including metrics like test coverage, test execution time, test case effectiveness, and test pass rate.

16.2.3 Quality Assurance Metrics

Quality assurance metrics, the bedrock of software quality engineering, unlock a treasure trove of invaluable insights into the software's overall health and the effectiveness of quality assurance processes. Like a compass guiding sailors across uncharted waters, these metrics navigate quality engineers through the complex landscape of quality assurance, helping them steer towards optimal outcomes and unparalleled excellence.

The significance of quality assurance metrics lies in their capacity to provide a quantitative and objective assessment of quality assurance efforts. Armed with meticulous data collection and analysis, quality engineers can gain a comprehensive understanding of the software's strengths, weaknesses, and areas requiring attention. With this newfound knowledge, they can chart a course toward data-driven decision-making, informed problem-solving, and strategic improvements.

At the heart of quality assurance metrics lies the Test Case Effectiveness metric, an illuminating lens into the quality and relevance of test cases. This metric serves as a litmus test, scrutinizing how well test cases align with the software's requirements and objectives.

A high test case effectiveness signaled the potency of the test cases in uncovering defects and validating the software's functionality, assuring stakeholders of the software's robustness. Quality assurance metrics assess the overall quality assurance process, such as the number of test cases created, test case execution status, and defect containment effectiveness.

CASE STUDY: UTILIZING QUALITY METRICS AT BELLOMY RESEARCH FOR SOFTWARE QUALITY IMPROVEMENT

We explore how **Bellomy Research** effectively implemented quality metrics to drive software quality improvements. By tracking defect density across different releases, they identified areas requiring attention and implemented targeted quality engineering practices, leading to a significant reduction in defects.

16.3 Data Analysis and Visualization Techniques

In the ever-evolving landscape of software quality engineering, the paramount significance of data analysis and visualization techniques cannot be overstated. As the volume and complexity of data continue to surge, these techniques emerge as essential tools, empowering quality engineers to glean actionable insights from the data deluge and make data-driven decisions with clarity and confidence. Effective data analysis and visualization play a crucial role in understanding quality metrics and making informed decisions.

16.3.1 Data Analysis Techniques

Data analysis techniques form the backbone of software quality engineering, harnessing the power of statistical analysis and trend exploration to unlock the hidden gems within quality metrics data. Like skilled detectives, quality engineers delve into the data's intricate web, ferreting out patterns, correlations, and anomalies that reveal the efficacy of their quality engineering practices. Statistical analysis emerges as a potential ally, equipping quality engineers with a suite of tools to understand the data's central tendencies, variations, and distributions. By wielding techniques such as mean, median, standard deviation, and hypothesis testing, they paint a vivid portrait of the data's landscape. Statistical analysis goes beyond mere summarization, empowering quality engineers to discern significant differences between groups and validate the impact of their quality initiatives with confidence and precision.

Trend analysis, another indispensable technique, sets quality engineers on a compelling journey of time-based exploration. By tracing the trajectories of quality metrics over time, they gain unparalleled insights into the software's performance and evolution. Upward trends signify progress and improvements in quality engineering practices, while downward trends prompt a deeper investigation into potential issues or setbacks. These trends act as beacons, guiding quality engineers towards continuous improvement and agile responses to emerging challenges.

Furthermore, correlation analysis reveals the intricate relationships between different quality metrics. By identifying correlations, quality engineers reveal the interplay between various factors that influence software quality. This knowledge enables them to focus their efforts on the most influential metrics, streamline their testing strategies, and optimize resource allocation.

16.3.2 *Visualization Techniques*

Visualization techniques in software quality engineering serve as powerful allies, transforming quality metrics data into visual masterpieces that are easily digestible and facilitate quick insights and data-driven decisions. Through the artful use of charts, graphs, and dashboards, quality engineers unlock the potential of visual representation to communicate complex information with clarity and impact. Charts, ranging from simple bar charts to intricate pie charts, offer a concise visual summary of quality metrics data. They allow quality engineers to compare different metrics, track progress over time, and identify patterns and trends at a glance. With a single glance at a well-crafted chart, stakeholders can swiftly absorb the essence of the data, enabling informed decision-making and fostering a shared understanding of the software's quality landscape. Visualization techniques, such as charts, graphs, and dashboards, present quality metrics data in a visual and easily understandable format, facilitating quick insights and data-driven decisions.

16.4 Types of Quality Metrics

Quality metrics serve as quantitative measures that provide insights into various dimensions of software development, enabling organizations to assess and enhance their processes, products, and user experiences. These metrics span a diverse range of aspects, each shedding light on different facets of software quality. Here are the key types of quality metrics commonly employed.

Process Metrics: Process metrics focus on evaluating the efficiency and effectiveness of software development processes. These metrics help organizations understand the health of their workflows and identify areas for improvement. Examples include the following:

- Cycle Time: The time taken to complete a specific task or process, indicating process efficiency.
- Lead Time: The time from the initiation of work to its completion, providing insights into overall process performance.
- Defect Arrival Rate: The rate at which defects are reported, highlighting process issues and potential bottlenecks.
- Code Review Turnaround Time: The time taken to review and approve code changes, reflecting the efficiency of code review processes.

Product Metrics: Product metrics assess the quality of the software product itself, including codebase, functionality, and reliability. These metrics offer insights into the overall robustness and user satisfaction of the software. Examples include the following:

- Code Complexity: Measures such as cyclomatic complexity that quantify the intricacy of the code, influencing maintainability and bug prevalence.
- Code Coverage: The percentage of code that is tested, indicating how well the codebase is covered by automated tests.

- Number of Defects: The count of reported defects, reflecting the software's stability and potential issues.
- Functionality Completeness: Measures the extent to which the software's features fulfill user requirements.

Project Metrics: Project metrics gauge the progress, scope, and health of a software development project. These metrics guide project management decisions and help ensure projects stay on track. Examples include the following:

- Schedule Variance: Compares actual project progress to the planned schedule, indicating whether the project is ahead or behind schedule.
- Budget Variance: Compares actual project costs to the budgeted costs, highlighting financial deviations.
- Scope Creep: Measures changes in project scope, signaling potential scope management challenges.
- Resource Utilization: Assesses the utilization of resources such as developers, testers, and infrastructure.

User Experience Metrics: User experience metrics focus on user satisfaction and engagement with the software. These metrics provide insights into the software's usability, performance, and overall value to users. Examples include the following:

- User Satisfaction (Net Promoter Score (NPS)): Measures user satisfaction and likelihood of recommending the software to others.
- User Engagement: Tracks user interactions, time spent using the software, and feature adoption rates.
- Response Time: Measures the time it takes for the software to respond to user interactions, impacting user experience.

Testing Metrics: Testing metrics evaluate the effectiveness and coverage of software testing activities. These metrics ensure that thorough testing is conducted to identify defects and ensure software reliability. Examples include the following:

- Test Coverage: Measures the extent to which the code is exercised by tests, indicating areas that need more comprehensive testing.

- Defect Detection Rate: The rate at which defects are identified during testing, reflecting the efficiency of testing efforts.
- Automated Test Execution Rate: Measures the percentage of tests that are automated, enhancing testing efficiency.

Each type of quality metric contributes to a holistic understanding of software quality, guiding decisions that lead to better products, efficient processes, and satisfied users. Organizations strategically select and employ these metrics to align with their goals, continuously improve their practices, and deliver software that meets the highest quality standards.

16.5 Key Performance Indicators (KPIS): Measuring Software Excellence and Progress

KPIs serve as essential benchmarks that quantify the effectiveness, efficiency, and overall health of software development processes and outcomes. These metrics provide organizations with actionable insights, enabling them to assess their progress, identify areas for improvement, and make informed decisions. "Code quality is intrinsically tied to the performance of a software application. High-quality code is optimized, efficient, and devoid of redundancies, ensuring that the software operates smoothly and responds swiftly to user inputs. When code is well-structured and follows established design patterns, it becomes easier to identify and rectify performance bottlenecks". The provided statement reinforces the connection between code quality and software performance, linking it to the broader context of KPIs in software development. It suggests that measuring and improving code quality can positively impact the key performance indicators that organizations use to assess the effectiveness, efficiency, and overall health of their software development processes and outcomes.

Here are the fundamental KPIs commonly utilized in software quality engineering.

Defect Density: Defect density measures the number of defects identified within a specific portion of the software code. It is calculated by dividing the total number of defects by the size of the codebase. This KPI indicates the software's quality level and helps identify code areas that require attention.

Code Churn: Code churn quantifies the amount of code that undergoes changes during a specific period, typically a sprint or release cycle. High code churn may indicate instability or frequent modifications, affecting development efficiency and quality.

Test Coverage: Test coverage measures the percentage of code that is exercised by tests. It provides insights into the thoroughness of testing efforts and highlights areas where testing might be insufficient, helping prevent potential defects.

Lead Time and Cycle Time: Lead time refers to the time taken to complete a task or feature from its initiation to deployment. Cycle time is the time it takes to move a feature or task from development to production. These KPIs reflect the efficiency of development processes and the overall project timeline.

Defect Escape Rate: The defect escape rate indicates the number of defects identified by users or customers after the software's release. A high defect escape rate suggests that the testing process might need enhancements to identify issues before release.

Mean Time to Detect (MTTD) and Mean Time to Resolve (MTTR): MTTD measures the average time taken to identify defects, while MTTR measures the average time to resolve them. These KPIs are crucial for gauging the efficiency of defect detection and resolution processes.

Customer Satisfaction and NPS: Customer satisfaction measures user contentment with the software, while NPS quantifies the likelihood of users recommending the software to others. These KPIs reflect the software's value to users and its alignment with user needs.

Velocity and Burn-Down Rate: Velocity measures the amount of work completed by a development team in a given sprint. Burn-down rate tracks the rate at which remaining work is being completed. These KPIs assist in Agile project management and planning.

Technical Debt: Technical debt quantifies the additional effort required in the future to address shortcuts or suboptimal solutions taken during development. This KPI highlights areas that might impact long-term software quality.

Continuous Integration and Deployment Frequency: These KPIs measure how frequently code is integrated and deployed to production. Higher integration and deployment frequencies promote continuous delivery practices and responsiveness to user needs.

Lead and Lag KPIs: Lead KPIs are proactive metrics that predict future performance, while lag KPIs are retrospective metrics that assess past performance. A balanced combination of both provides a comprehensive view of software development effectiveness.

By strategically selecting and monitoring these KPIs, organizations gain insights into their software quality, development processes, and user satisfaction. These metrics facilitate data-driven decision-making, promote continuous improvement, and ensure that software products meet the highest standards of excellence.

16.6 Balancing Quantitative and Qualitative Measures: Striking Harmony in Software Assessment

Effective software assessment encompasses both quantitative and qualitative measures, each offering distinct perspectives on quality. Balancing these dimensions ensures a comprehensive understanding of software performance and user satisfaction. While quantitative metrics provide numerical insights, qualitative measures offer valuable contextual information. Striking a balance allows organizations to make informed decisions and optimize software quality holistically.

16.7 Metrics-Driven Decision-Making

Leverages data-backed insights to guide actions and strategies in software development. By analyzing relevant metrics, organizations gain a deeper understanding of software quality, process efficiency, and user experiences. This approach enables informed choices that align with project goals, enhance practices, and deliver value to users. Metrics-driven decision-making transforms data into actionable steps, fostering continuous improvement and driving success.

16.8 Metrics Challenges and Pitfalls: Navigating the Path to Accurate Measurement

While metrics offer valuable insights, they also present challenges and pitfalls that require careful navigation.

- Metric Overload: Measuring too many metrics can lead to information overload, making it challenging to focus on what truly matters.
- Inappropriate Metrics: Selecting metrics without aligning them to project objectives or user needs can result in irrelevant or misleading insights.
- Gaming the System: Teams might prioritize metrics over actual quality, leading to behaviors that inflate metrics without improving software quality.
- Misinterpretation: Misinterpreting metrics or failing to consider their context can result in misguided decisions.
- Lack of Context: Quantitative metrics might lack the context necessary to fully understand their implications.
- Data Integrity: Poor data quality or inconsistent data collection can undermine the accuracy of metrics.
- Short-Term Focus: Focusing solely on short-term metrics might lead to neglecting long-term software quality goals.

Navigating these challenges requires a thoughtful approach. Organizations must define clear objectives, choose relevant metrics, and continuously evaluate their effectiveness. Open communication, collaboration, and a willingness to adapt are essential to successfully leverage metrics for improved decision-making and software excellence.

CASE STUDY:ENHANCED DECISION-MAKING AT ADORIASOFT THROUGH DATA ANALYSIS AND VISUALIZATION

We examined how Adoriasoft utilized data analysis and visualization techniques to improve their understanding of quality metrics and drive quality improvements. A real-time dashboard displaying key quality metrics enabled stakeholders to monitor quality initiatives' progress and address areas of concern promptly.

Practical Exercise:

You can perform a quality metrics analysis exercise with these steps.

- Identify relevant quality metrics for your software project, such as defect density or test coverage.
- Collect and verify the necessary data.
- Apply appropriate data analysis techniques, such as trend analysis or correlation analysis, to gain insights from the metric data.
- Visualize the metrics data using suitable techniques, like charts or graphs, to facilitate effective communication and decision-making.

17

Agile and Lean Practices for Software Quality Engineering

17.1 Agile Development Principles

Agile software development stands as a revolutionary paradigm that has transformed the software industry, reshaping the way software products are conceived, developed, and delivered. At its core, Agile champions collaboration, flexibility, and iterative development, propelling teams towards higher levels of efficiency, responsiveness, and customer satisfaction. In this section, we embark on a journey to explore the key principles of Agile and their profound impact on quality engineering.

17.1.1 Iterative and Incremental Development

Agile stands tall as an unwavering advocate for the power of iterative and incremental methodologies. Embracing this dynamic approach, developers embark on an exhilarating journey of crafting software piece by piece, sprint by sprint. The heartbeat of Agile lies in its short and focused development cycles, aptly named sprints, where innovation takes flight and progress dances hand in hand with efficiency. Amidst this dynamic landscape, quality engineering emerges as the stalwart companion of Agile, harmoniously syncing with its core principles. Akin to an artistic dance partner, quality engineering embarks on a continuous tango of testing and validation throughout each and every sprint. Unleashing its prowess, it ensures that each fragment of code is subjected to the rigorous examination of perfection. With Agile's wings carrying the project forward in leaps and bounds, the concept of stagnation becomes an alien notion.

In the heart of this ever-transforming landscape, quality engineering weaves its threads of vigilance into the fabric of every sprint. Like a vigilant sentinel, it guards against the encroachment of bugs and defects, sparing no effort to fortify the foundations of the software masterpiece. By intertwining its web of verification and validation throughout the entire development journey, it nurtures a culture of excellence that is inscribed in the very DNA of the project.

17.1.2 Customer Collaboration

Customer collaboration stands as an indispensable cornerstone, serving as the compass that navigates the software development voyage toward customer satisfaction. With open channels of communication, Agile welcomes the invaluable insights and feedback of customers, recognizing that their perspective holds the key to crafting software that truly resonates with their expectations. By actively engaging customers and stakeholders, quality engineering fosters an environment of collaboration, where their voices are not only heard but celebrated. This symbiotic relationship between development and customers breathes life into the software, endowing it with the essence of genuine user-centricity.

Customers become integral participants in the process, invited to embark on the exhilarating adventure of exploration and refinement. Armed with a plethora of testing methodologies, quality engineering empowers customers to put the software through its paces, unearthing both its strengths and areas for improvement. Customer feedback becomes a precious gem, illuminating the path towards excellence.

17.1.3 Self-Organizing Teams

Agile philosophy lies in the empowerment of self-organizing teams, where individual talents converge to create a collective force that propels the project toward success. Within this collaborative tapestry, the notion of quality becomes a shared responsibility that intertwines the efforts of every team member, each contributing their unique expertise and passion.

Quality engineers stand shoulder to shoulder with developers, testers, and all team members, forging an unbreakable bond of partnership. Their role is not one of mere oversight or detachment but rather of active engagement and integration. Quality engineers, like master weavers, bring their domain knowledge and meticulous eye for detail to the table, infusing each phase of the development process with a sense of precision. They collaborate closely with developers, providing insights and guidance on best practices, enhancing code quality, and fostering a culture of continuous improvement.

17.2 Quality Assurance in Agile Projects

Quality assurance practices in Agile projects form the very bedrock upon which successful software development endeavors thrive. Within this dynamic landscape, quality engineering emerges as a pivotal force, actively shaping and fortifying the project's path to triumph. Let us venture into this realm of excellence and explore how Agile's quality assurance practices, supported by the prowess of quality engineering, weave a tale of unrivaled success. Unlike traditional approaches, this section delves into quality assurance practices in Agile projects and how quality engineering contributes to their overall success.

17.2.1 Agile Testing Techniques

Agile testing techniques, such as exploratory testing and test-driven development, play a critical role in ensuring software quality in the fast-paced Agile environment. Quality engineers are instrumental in applying these techniques effectively.

17.2.2 Continuous Integration and Testing

Continuous integration (CI) and continuous testing are fundamental Agile practices. Quality engineers work closely with developers to integrate automated tests into the CI pipeline, enabling frequent and efficient testing. CI and continuous testing form the backbone of a highly efficient and quality-driven software development process. These fundamental practices are like a well-choreographed dance, harmoniously blending the efforts of developers and quality engineers to achieve a seamless and automated testing experience. CI is a process that brings together the work of multiple developers into a shared repository on a regular basis. This integration not only promotes collaboration but also serves as the foundation for frequent and automated testing. With each code commit, the CI pipeline springs to life, automating the build and testing processes.

Quality engineers, like skilled partners in this dance, work closely with developers to weave a tapestry of automated tests. These automated tests are then meticulously integrated into the CI pipeline, ensuring they become an integral part of the development process.

CASE STUDY: QUALITY ASSURANCE IN AGILE AT AGILE INNOVATIONS CO.

In this case study, we explore how **Agile Innovations Co.** effectively implemented quality assurance practices within their Agile projects, resulting in high-quality software releases. By embracing Agile testing techniques and involving quality engineers in cross-functional Agile teams, Agile Innovations Co. successfully integrated test automation into their CI pipeline, leading to rapid feedback and quick defect detection.

17.3 Lean Principles and Quality Improvement

Lean principles focus on eliminating waste, optimizing processes, and continuously improving quality. This section examines how quality engineering aligns with Lean principles for quality improvement.

17.3.1 Waste Reduction

Waste reduction is a critical aspect of quality engineering in software development. The concept of waste comes from Lean principles, which originated in manufacturing but have been widely adapted to software development as well. Waste refers to any activity, process, or resource that doesn't add value to the end product or the customer. Identifying and eliminating waste leads to more efficient and effective development processes, ultimately resulting in higher-quality software and a better overall development experience. Quality engineering plays a pivotal role in identifying and eliminating waste in the software development process, such as unnecessary rework, inefficient testing procedures, or redundant documentation. By minimizing waste, the focus is redirected towards delivering high-quality software.

17.3.2 Value Stream Mapping (VSM)

VSM is a lean management technique used to analyze and visualize the flow of materials, information, and activities required to deliver a product or service to the end customer. It is a powerful tool for identifying waste, inefficiencies, and opportunities for improvement within a process. While it originated in manufacturing, VSM has been adapted and widely used in software development and other knowledge work domains. VSM is used to identify and eliminate non-value-added activities, thereby streamlining the process and improving overall efficiency and quality. By providing a holistic view of the entire value stream, it helps teams and organizations understand how value is created, identify bottlenecks, and uncover opportunities for process optimization. Quality engineering actively participates in VSM exercises, identifying bottlenecks and areas for quality improvement.

17.3.3 Kaizen and Continuous Improvement

The concept of Kaizen, or continuous improvement, is intrinsic to Lean principles. Quality engineers actively contribute to process improvements, utilizing techniques like root cause analysis and process optimization to enhance software quality.

CASE STUDY: LEAN QUALITY IMPROVEMENT AT VISIONARY ENTERPRISES LTD.

In this case study, we explore how **Visionary Enterprises Ltd.** embraced Lean principles to drive quality improvement through effective quality engineering practices. By implementing VSM, Visionary Enterprises Ltd. identified areas of waste and inefficiency. Quality engineers played a key role in optimizing testing processes and improving overall software quality.

18

THE FUTURE OF SOFTWARE
QUALITY ENGINEERING

18.1 Trends and Innovations in Quality Engineering

The field of software quality engineering is ever-evolving, with emerging trends and innovations shaping its future. The dynamic realm of software quality engineering is a captivating voyage of perpetual transformation, where pioneering trends and ground-breaking innovations unfurl the pathway to its promising future. As technology's unstoppable march continues, quality engineering adapts and evolves, embracing novel methodologies to conquer the challenges and seize the opportunities of the digital landscape.

18.1.1 Test Automation and AI/ML Integration

Test automation is advancing rapidly, with increased integration of artificial intelligence (AI) and machine learning (ML) techniques. AI/ML-powered testing tools can analyze vast amounts of data, identify patterns, and make intelligent decisions, thereby enhancing testing efficiency and effectiveness.

18.1.2 Shift-Left Testing

The concept of "shift-left" testing stands as a transformative force, reshaping the very foundations of the development process. This paradigm shift involves the strategic integration of testing activities at the earliest stages of the software development lifecycle, heralding a new era of proactivity and efficiency.

By infusing quality engineering practices from the outset, organizations embark on a journey of early detection and resolution. As code begins to take shape, quality engineers collaborate seamlessly with developers, conducting a symphony of tests to scrutinize the

DOI: 10.1201/9781032702049-18

evolving software. This proactive approach enables the swift identification of potential defects and issues, catching them before they can
take root and fester.

This not only saves valuable time and resources but also fosters an
environment of continuous improvement and responsiveness. Shift-left
testing not only enhances efficiency but also plays a pivotal role in
elevating overall software quality. By addressing issues at their infancy,
organizations ensure that the end product is resilient, reliable, and
tailored to meet the precise needs of the end users. The seamless
collaboration between quality engineers and developers nurtures a culture
of shared responsibility where quality becomes a collective pursuit.

18.1.3 DevSecOps

The seamless integration of security practices into the DevOps approach
is gaining significant traction in the world of software development.
Quality engineering stands as a pivotal force in ensuring software
security by diligently implementing robust security testing, conducting
thorough vulnerability assessments, and advocating secure coding
practices throughout the entire development lifecycle. This approach
fosters a proactive and collaborative mindset where security is not an
afterthought but an inherent aspect of the software creation process. By
addressing potential vulnerabilities early on and continuously, organizations fortify their software against potential threats, enhancing its
resilience and reliability. The cohesive blend of security practices within
DevOps culture creates a fortified foundation, instilling confidence in
the software's ability to withstand cyber threats and adhere to ever-
evolving cybersecurity standards. Through the combined efforts of
DevSecOps and quality engineering, organizations pave the way for a
future where software security is not a mere checkbox but a steadfast
commitment to safeguarding the digital landscape.

18.1.4 Quality Engineering at Scale

Agile practices are expanding beyond individual teams to large-
scale Agile implementations. Quality engineering must adapt to
support Agile at scale, addressing challenges such as coordination,
integration, and ensuring consistent quality across multiple teams.

18.2 Continuous Learning and Professional Development

In the rapidly evolving world of software quality engineering, continuous learning and professional development are essential for future success. As technology advances and industry demands evolve, quality engineers must embrace a mindset of lifelong learning to stay ahead. Continuous learning allows them to stay abreast of the latest advancements, industry trends, and emerging best practices. Professional development activities such as workshops, seminars, and certifications provide practical experience and opportunities for networking with industry peers. By acquiring specialized skills in areas like security testing and test automation, quality engineers become valuable assets to their organizations. Organizations that prioritize the growth and development of their quality engineering teams gain a competitive edge by delivering high-quality software products. By embracing a growth mindset and investing in continuous learning, quality engineers navigate the ever-changing landscape of software development with confidence and expertise.

18.2.1 Keeping Abreast of Technological Advancements

Quality engineers must continuously seek to expand their knowledge by staying updated with the latest technologies, tools, and methodologies. Through continuous learning, they can gain valuable insights into emerging trends, evaluate new testing approaches, and harness innovative tools to enhance software quality. Embracing this proactive approach, quality engineers equip themselves with the skills and expertise needed to tackle evolving challenges and deliver cutting-edge solutions. By keeping abreast of technological advancements, they become instrumental in driving success and excellence in the ever-changing landscape of software development.

18.2.2 Industry Certifications and Training Programs

Industry certifications and training programs hold immense value for quality engineers, elevating their expertise and credibility within the competitive landscape of software development. Pursuing reputable certifications, such as the International Software Testing Qualifications

Board certification, signifies a commitment to excellence and adherence to global standards of software testing. These certifications serve as a testament to quality engineers' proficiency and dedication, providing tangible evidence of their competence to prospective employers and clients. They showcase a comprehensive understanding of fundamental testing principles and best practices, further solidifying their reputation as skilled professionals in the field. Participating in specialized training programs on specific tools or methodologies enhances a quality engineer's versatility and adaptability. As technology evolves, mastering tools and techniques becomes pivotal to navigating the intricate intricacies of modern software testing. By honing their expertise in automation frameworks, security testing, performance testing, or other niche areas, quality engineers open doors to exciting career opportunities and projects.

Industry certifications and training programs can lead to increased job prospects, salary advancements, and career growth. Employers recognize the value of qualified and certified quality engineers, and they are more likely to invest in individuals who showcase a commitment to continuous improvement. Beyond personal benefits, certified quality engineers contribute significantly to their organizations by ensuring that software quality remains a top priority. Armed with comprehensive knowledge and recognized credentials, they become instrumental in elevating the overall quality of products and services, instilling trust in customers and stakeholders.

18.2.3 Networking and Community Engagement

Engaging with professional networks and communities fosters knowledge sharing, collaboration, and exposure to diverse perspectives. Quality engineers can join industry forums, attend conferences, and participate in local meetups to expand their network and learn from peers.

18.2.4 Continuous Improvement and Skill Development

Actively seeking opportunities for continuous improvement and skill development, such as attending Workshops, webinars, and conferences, as well as participating in hackathons and open-source projects, helps quality engineers stay at the forefront of their field.

By embracing continuous learning and professional development, quality engineers can adapt to the ever-changing landscape of software quality engineering and contribute to future advancements in the field.

18.3 Conclusion: A Comprehensive Guide to Software Quality Engineering

This book has provided a thorough and comprehensive understanding of software quality engineering concepts and practices. From foundational principles to advanced topics, real-world case studies, practical examples, and interactive exercises, we have explored a wide array of aspects within quality engineering. By applying these principles and embracing emerging trends, quality engineers can ensure the delivery of high-quality software that meets and exceeds customer expectations. The future of software quality engineering is brimming with exciting possibilities, and it is our responsibility as quality professionals to drive innovation and contribute to the ongoing improvement of software quality.

Throughout this book, we have embarked on a journey through the vast and intricate domain of software quality engineering. Starting with a firm grasp of the fundamentals, we delved into various critical areas, such as testing, test planning, automation, performance, security, usability, and more. Through detailed explanations, compelling case studies, illustrative examples, and engaging practical exercises, our aim has been to provide readers with a comprehensive understanding of software quality engineering concepts and practices.

A recurring theme in each chapter has been the indispensable role of software quality engineering in the software development lifecycle. We have witnessed how quality engineering is a key player in ensuring that software meets customer expectations, performs optimally, and is resilient against security threats. By seamlessly integrating quality engineering practices at every stage of the software development process, organizations can deliver reliable, high-quality software that enhances customer satisfaction and builds trust.

Moreover, we explored the vital role of quality engineering in Agile, Lean, and DevOps environments. These innovative methodologies have revolutionized software development, and quality engineering has adapted accordingly to cater to their evolving needs. Agile, with its emphasis on collaboration, iterative development, and customer feedback, has a natural synergy with quality engineering. Lean's focus on waste reduction and continuous improvement aligns seamlessly with quality engineering's goals. In the realm of DevOps, quality engineering plays a crucial role in tightly integrating testing and deployment pipelines, enabling continuous testing, and ensuring a seamless software release process.

As we move forward, we delve into emerging trends and innovations shaping the future of software quality engineering. We examined the integration of AI and ML techniques, the shift towards shift-left testing, the adoption of DevSecOps practices, and the scaling of Agile methodologies, among other developments. To thrive in this ever-changing landscape, quality engineers must embrace continuous learning and professional development. Staying up to date with technological advancements, acquiring industry certifications, engaging with professional networks, and actively seeking opportunities for skill enhancement are key to remaining at the forefront of this field.

In closing, we must recognize the vital role that software quality engineering plays in the success of software projects. By adhering to quality engineering practices, organizations can mitigate risks, reduce defects, improve efficiency, and ultimately deliver software products that meet or surpass customer expectations. Software quality engineering is not a one-time effort but an ongoing commitment to excellence. It demands collaboration, dedication, and continuous improvement. As quality professionals, it is our responsibility to drive innovation, foster a culture of quality, and contribute to the ongoing advancement of software quality engineering.

We hope this comprehensive guide has provided you with valuable insights, knowledge, and practical guidance to elevate your understanding of software quality engineering. By implementing the concepts and practices presented herein, you are well-equipped to embark on your journey as a software quality engineer, ensuring the delivery of high-quality software that leaves a positive impact on the world.

Glossary

Agile: is an iterative and incremental software development methodology that emphasizes collaboration, adaptability, and customer-centricity.

Automation: is the process of using tools or software programs to execute repetitive tasks or tests with minimal human intervention, enhancing efficiency and accuracy.

Code Review: A critical examination of software code to identify and rectify issues, improve code quality, and ensure adherence to coding standards.

Continuous Integration (CI): is a development practice that frequently integrates code changes into a shared repository, followed by automated builds and tests to detect integration issues early in the development process.

Defect: An anomaly or flaw in software that deviates from its intended behavior or specifications, requiring resolution to ensure desired functionality.

DevOps: A cultural and operational approach that unifies development (Dev) and operations (Ops) teams, fostering collaboration and automating the software delivery process.

Quality Assurance (QA): A comprehensive set of activities and processes aimed at ensuring that software meets predefined quality standards and fulfills user requirements.

Root Cause Analysis (RCA): A systematic investigation process is used to identify the underlying causes of problems or defects in software or processes, facilitating targeted resolutions.

Software Development Life Cycle (SDLC): A structured approach to software development encompassing all phases, from initial requirements gathering to deployment and maintenance.

Test Case: A specific set of actions or conditions, along with expected results, is used to assess the functionality and correctness of a particular software feature.

Test Plan: A detailed document outlining the approach, objectives, resources, and schedule for a software testing project, providing a roadmap for successful testing execution.

Test Strategy: A high-level plan defining the overall testing approach, scope, objectives, and resource allocation for a software testing effort.

Usability: The measure of how user-friendly and easy-to-use software is, including factors such as user interface design, navigation, and the overall user experience.

Vulnerability: Weaknesses or flaws in software that can be exploited to compromise its security, integrity, or availability, requiring timely identification and mitigation.

These definitions offer a fundamental understanding of commonly used terms in the field of software quality engineering. It is essential to note that some terms may have nuanced meanings depending on the context and industry. Continuous learning and practical experience will deepen your understanding of these concepts and their application in real-world scenarios.

Bibliography

Black, R. (2009). *Managing the testing process* (pp. 87). Wiley.

Clokie, K. (2017). *A practical guide to testing in DevOps* (pp. 28). Lean Publication.

Crispin, L., & Gregory, J. (2009). *Agile testing: A practical guide for testers and agile teams* (pp. 271). Addison-Wesley.

Crispin, L., & Gregory, J. (2009). *Agile testing: A practical guide for testers and agile teams* (pp. 418). Addison-Wesley.

Crispin, L., & Gregory, J. (2009). *Agile testing: A practical guide for testers and agile teams* (pp. 471). Addison-Wesley.

Hewage, R. (2020, March 28). *What is DevOps?* Medium. https://levelup.gitconnected.com/what-is-devops-393eed56dea2

Kaner, C. (2012). *Testing computer software* (pp. 233). Wiley.

Laboon, B. (2017). *Friendly introduction to software testing* (pp. 11). Create space.

Laboon, B. (2017). *Friendly introduction to software testing* (pp. 13). Create space.

Mili, A. (2015). *Software testing: Concepts and operations* (pp. 38). Wiley.

Myers, G. J., Sandler, C., & Badgett, T. (2012). *The art of software testing* (3rd ed., pp. 5). John Wiley & Sons.

Myers, G. J., Sandler, C., & Badgett, T. (2012). *The art of software testing* (3rd ed., pp. 160). John Wiley & Sons.

Pargaonkar, S. (2023). "A comprehensive review of performance testing methodologies and best practices: Software quality engineering", *International Journal of Science and Research*, Volume 12, Issue 8, pp. 2008–2014. https://www.ijsr.net/getabstract.php?paperid=SR23822111402

Pargaonkar, S. (2023). "Advancements in security testing: A comprehensive review of methodologies and emerging trends in software quality engineering",

International Journal of Science and Research, Volume 12, Issue 9, pp. 61–66. https://www.ijsr.net/getabstract.php?paperid=SR23829090815

Pargaonkar, S. (2023). "Cultivating software excellence: The intersection of code quality and dynamic analysis in contemporary software development within the field of software quality engineering", *International Journal of Science and Research*, Volume 12, Issue 9, pp. 10–13. https://www.ijsr.net/getabstract.php?paperid=SR23829092346

Pargaonkar, S. (2023). "Enhancing software quality in architecture design: A survey- based approach", *International Journal of Scientific and Research Publications*, Volume 13, Issue 8 (ISSN: 2250-3153). 10.29322/IJSRP.13.08.2023.p14014

SDLC – Spiral model. Online Tutorials, Courses, and eBooks Library. (2). https://www.tutorialspoint.com/sdlc/sdlc_spiral_model.html

V-model (software engineering) – Javatpoint. www.javatpoint.com. (n.d.). https://www.javatpoint.com/software-engineering-v-model

Printed in the United States
by Baker & Taylor Publisher Services